D0787033

Praise for
Outlove: A Queer Christian Survival Story

"Julie Rodgers's wisdom, clarity, and voice have been saving lives for a long while. *Outlove* will heal broken hearts, families, and entire communities."

—Glennon Doyle, author of the #1 bestseller
Untamed and founder of Together Rising

"Julie's personal story is a wake-up call for anyone who believes that the harmful practice of conversion therapy is a thing of the past. Her journey will give you hope for who we can become and will inspire you to be a larger part of an overdue urgent movement for change."

—Cory Booker, US Senator and
former Democratic presidential candidate

"Julie Rodgers recounts her escape from this toxic system of heartbreak and trauma with integrity and an otherworldly level of grace that will inspire readers to rejoice in how perfectly God made our LGBTQ+ siblings."

—Kirsten Powers, CNN Senior Political
Analyst and *USA Today* columnist

"A powerful and unflinching memoir about how love can save us. And must."

—Kate Bowler, professor at Duke University and bestselling
author of *Everything Happens for a Reason (And Other Lies I've Loved)*

"Brave, candid, beautifully vulnerable—this book is a gift, and so is Julie. Her journey hasn't been easy, yet her courageous witness and inspiring perseverance beckon us back to the healing beauty of God's irrepressible love."

—Jeff Chu, author of *Does Jesus Really Love Me?*
and co-curator of Evolving Faith

OUTLOVE

A QUEER CHRISTIAN
SURVIVAL STORY

JULIE RODGERS

Broadleaf Books
Minneapolis

OUTLOVE
A Queer Christian Survival Story

Scriptures taken from the Holy Bible, New International Version®, NIV®.
Copyright © 1973, 1978, 1984, 2011 by Biblica, Inc.™ Used by permission
of Zondervan. All rights reserved worldwide. www.zondervan.com The
"NIV" and "New International Version" are trademarks registered in the
United States Patent and Trademark Office by Biblica, Inc.™

Outlove is a work of nonfiction. Some names and details have been changed
to protect the privacy of people in the stories. Events and dialogue are
constructed from memory.

Cover design: Faceout Studios

Print ISBN: 978-1-5064-6404-6
eBook ISBN: 978-1-5064-6405-3

CONTENTS

CONTENTS

PART III

AUTHOR'S NOTE

This is a work of creative nonfiction. We should acknowledge upfront that my memory is imperfect, and my perspective is subjective. In each of these stories, I tried my best to capture the spirit of what was said in dialogue, relying on memory, emails, and speeches, but statements presented as quotations in what follows necessarily are often not verbatim. While all of the stories are true, based on real people I've known and loved, I altered details about many of them to protect their privacy.

I imagine some of the people in these stories have a different perspective from what I share here, just as adult siblings have conflicting recollections of childhood memories. In those cases, I welcome other viewpoints. Far from negating the truth, their perspectives would illuminate the events and add layers to the meaning of what happened.

It's really hard being human, and most of us are doing the best we can. Even when particular incidents that I describe don't reflect positively on certain characters, I hope their humanity comes through.

PART I

I was fresh out of college, six years into my journey toward freedom from homosexuality, and I was still super gay. In the fourth-row, center-aisle seat at Living Hope's weekly support group for people who struggled with same-sex attractions, I listened to Ricky Chelette, the executive director of Living Hope Ministries, preach a message about a parable in the Gospel of Luke.

In the story, a son asks his father for his inheritance while his dad is still alive. Then the son goes to a far-off place and parties the money away. One day, after squandering his wealth, he wakes up in a literal pigsty and realizes he can go home. The whole way home, he prepares a speech for his father. He imagines himself falling at his father's feet, pleading for forgiveness. He resolves to offer himself as a servant in his father's house, where the servants—enslaved people—had a nice life compared to the ruins he faced in the faraway land. When the son finally turns the corner onto the road that ends at his father's house, he's stunned to see his father standing on the porch, looking down the road, awaiting his return. His dad runs to him, throws his coat around him, and wraps him up in his arms. The son falls to the ground to beg for mercy, but his father pulls him right back up, embracing him and weeping. Then he tells his servants to slay a fattened calf and prepare to throw a party—his lost son had come home (Luke 15:11–32).

"Some of the people I love most in the world have followed in the footsteps of the prodigal son," Ricky said to the roughly one hundred of us in the audience who were seeking healing for our same-sex attractions. "They've chosen to give in to their flesh, to turn away from the truth and embrace a debaucherous lifestyle."

I thought about my friends from the ministry who had come and gone. Many of my closest friends had recently been kicked out after they broke one of Living Hope's golden rules: no outside contact. We weren't allowed to talk to each other without supervision because Living Hope leaders feared we would meet up and have sex. The ones I was still connected to looked nothing like the prodigal son Ricky described. They were seminary graduates, Sunday school teachers, earnest seekers. Far from having "gone to the dark side," as Ricky described them, some of them still hadn't had their first kiss.

"Just like the father in this story," Ricky continued, "I'm standing on the porch with my arms wide open, waiting for my beloved friends, many of whom are like sons and daughters, to come to the end of themselves and return home."

I was one of the people Ricky loved like his own kid. Sent to Living Hope when I came out as a teenager, I practically grew up in the ministry. I was at Living Hope's support group on Thursday nights and the healing prayer group on Tuesdays. I lived with Ricky and his wife for a few months and in Living Hope's recovery house for a couple of years. I ate lunch at Ricky's every Sunday afternoon. I was his go-to dog-sitter, his ride home from the airport, his protégé, and his first pick to give my testimony before he spoke to churches about hope for healing from homosexuality. Where I come from, good kids aren't gay, and all I wanted was to be good.

What a horror, then, to listen to Ricky's sermon about the prodigal son, fully aware that I was still a lesbian. What's a queer person to do in that situation, when the only people we've ever known and loved believe our love is disordered and our bodies are broken? How does someone in their midtwenties, whose brain is still developing and who's never known life outside of fundamentalism, begin to imagine an honest and integrated life? Was there any other way for me to be good, a way that didn't require me to shut down, suppress, fragment, and annihilate integral parts of myself to belong?

"We serve a Father in heaven who longs to throw us a party," Ricky said to close out his sermon. "All we have to do is come to the end of ourselves and come home. So here's my question to those of you who might be in the far-off place tonight: Are you ready to come home?"

In the eyes of my community, I was home. I was denying myself, which meant no sex, love, or intimacy with women—no handholding, no snuggling, no kissing, no fantasizing, no daydreaming about creating a life with a loving partner. That night, though, I couldn't help wondering, *At what cost?* And was it really *me* who was home, or was it the image of myself I presented in order to fit into a religious system that either couldn't or wouldn't make room for queer people who told the truth about themselves? In the years that followed, I often thought, *Maybe they just don't understand. Maybe if someone like me told the truth about myself and stayed in the Evangelical church, they would see the humanity of queer people and be moved to embrace us. Maybe we could grow in love together.*

2

My mother converted to Christianity when my oldest brother was a toddler. She probably wouldn't describe it as a conversion if she were telling this story, though. She'd say she *got saved.* She would say she had been utterly lost, given to blackout drinking, waking up in her car with no memory of the night before, and then she found Jesus, and everything changed. She quit drinking. She quit smoking. She joined a weekly Bible study that forbade her from seeing R-rated movies. Eventually, she dragged my father to the neighborhood Baptist church in their suburb of Houston, setting the pace for their new rhythms as a growing family. Gone were the days when she lived in darkness, when she lived according to the desires of her flesh. She was a new creation.

"I wanted to be a good mom more than anything else in the world," I remember her saying in my earliest memories. "When Michael was born, I looked around and thought, *The good moms take their kids to church!* So I took him to church, and I met Jesus."

My mom immediately found a place to belong in the neighborhood church. Suddenly, she had a group of women she could call upon when she was in need—women who brought casseroles when she was sick and sent encouraging cards when she was sad. She had walking buddies and prayer partners. She found mentors in the church, wise elders who were eager to nurture her spiritual growth. And in this lonely world, where many of us suffer in silence, that kind of intimacy is a healing balm.

Before she became a Christian, she felt lost when it came to questions of meaning and morality. Now she had a moral framework that told her exactly how to be good.

The year before my mom became a Christian, Jerry Falwell founded the Moral Majority with the express purpose of mobilizing conservative Christians to rally behind a Republican political platform. Two years before that, James Dobson started Focus on the Family with the mission of "nurturing and defending the God-ordained institution of the family." My mom looked to leaders on the Christian Right for moral guidance and answers to the many questions she brought to Christianity. They told her what was right and what was wrong, who was good and who was bad. The enemies were the feminists, the gays, the liberals, and the people who wanted to keep prayer out of public schools. By the time I came along, six years after she became a Christian, my mom was deeply fearful of secular influences on her children.

My mom prayed for me from the day she learned she was pregnant. With joy and anticipation, she prayed for a baby girl who would grow to love the Lord. She prayed for my future husband, believing God already knew the boy who would one day be my rock and my protector, the man I would joyfully submit to as the leader of my future household. In preparation for her first and only daughter, she read books from Focus on the Family that told her how to raise little girls who would grow into godly women—the kind of women who taught children's church or women's Bible studies, who served God by serving their families. She pleaded with God to guard me from the ways of the world. She believed she was put on this earth for one purpose: to raise children who would become ambassadors for Christ.

My dad didn't share my mom's enthusiasm for Evangelical Christianity. His father had been a stern fundamentalist Christian, and my dad found their religious community to be so intolerable that he left home to join the army at seventeen years old. It was always difficult to imagine my dad in the military: with soft, gray hair and a slender frame, he moved through the world slowly, cheerfully, with a sense of wonder. He was a high school history teacher, and he processed new information with patience and curiosity. When conservative Christians railed against "those people," whoever they happened to be, my dad saw complex people with complicated histories who were doing the best they could in a difficult world. Where fundamentalists gave answers, my dad wanted room for mystery. Where they saw black and white, he noticed endless shades of gray. But my dad also strived to maintain harmony in his relationships, avoiding conflict at all cost, so when my mom decided they were going to immerse themselves in Evangelical Christianity, he went with the flow. He sang worship songs on Sundays, attended weekly men's Bible studies, and kept his opinions to himself.

My mom sent me to kindergarten at a local Christian school so I would learn to read, and then she homeschooled me up until high school. We didn't do much schoolwork, though. My older brother Kenny and I watched *Matlock* every morning at 10:05 a.m. and four episodes of *Saved by the Bell* every afternoon. We played basketball in our driveway between shows and occasionally snuck in forbidden secular music videos on MTV. The goal of homeschooling was to keep us away from the gays and goth kids, to guard us from science teachers who would teach evolution and tell us God did not create the earth six thousand years ago. My mom believed that science and history lessons from worldly teachers were of no use to us; we only needed to study the Bible. With the sword of God's truth in our hands, we would be equipped with all the knowledge we needed to be God's representatives here on earth.

It's tempting for people to dismiss that kind of sheltered, religious upbringing with a smug sense of superiority, but that doesn't do justice to the emotional and spiritual needs it met. I was happy. I was moved by the Christian message. Who doesn't want to have a grand mission in life, to lose themselves in a sweeping story of redemption and restoration?

I made some friends through basketball leagues and Sunday school classes, but my best friends were my mom and my brother Kenny. Our neighborhood was a fifteen-minute drive outside of Tomball, Texas, which had a population of about one thousand people when I was a kid. We would drive "into town" in my mom's maroon Suburban with the windows down, blasting the golden oldies—the only exception to our rule against secular music. With no musical talent and no shame, my mom and I belted out songs with the Beach Boys, the Beatles, and Sonny and Cher. We took special trips to our favorite snow-cone stand during hot Texas summers. We drove all over the state together for my basketball tournaments. We laughed and we sang and we talked about Jesus. Most days I felt like we had everything we needed in my mom's maroon Suburban: large Dr Peppers, carefree spirits, and seemingly unbreakable bonds with one another.

By the time I was eight years old, I had learned that I was a sinner and that the punishment for sinners like me was eternal damnation. I believed hell was a physical place that existed somewhere beneath the earth and that I would burn in a lake of fire for eternity if I did not commit my life to Jesus. I ingested the message slowly, through activities like arts-and-crafts time at children's church, where teachers helped us make colorful bracelets and then explained how the different colors stood for hell, or our sin, or the blood of Jesus, which they said could wash us clean if only we believed. On an uneventful afternoon in our two-story house in Tomball, I knelt beside my mom on the beige carpet of her bathroom floor and repeated a prayer after her. I told God I was sorry for all of my sins, and I asked Jesus to come into my heart. When I got up from the bathroom floor, I didn't know if I was changed, but one thing I knew for sure: I had made my mother proud.

At some point, my faith took on a life of its own. I didn't know if Jesus lived in my heart, but I knew that if Jesus had lived in my neighborhood, he would have been my friend. I loved how Jesus paid attention to children in the Bible stories we read. I was moved by the way he treated people who weren't wanted in their communities. I noticed he treated them with dignity. If Jesus liked the people in the Bible who couldn't quite measure up to their community's expectations, I thought, then maybe he would like me too.

o o o

I realized I might be gay when I was ten years old, and I was sure of it once I was invited to middle school sleepovers. Those nights were this homeschooler's sexual awakening: I traced the outline of my friend Rachel's lips when she read Bible verses. My stomach dropped, the way it did on a roller coaster, when Natalie sat close to me on the couch. It was a thrilling time—to feel so alive and connected to my body—but I didn't feel comfortable telling the people around me.

"Gay people are an abomination," my mom would say to me in casual moments, like on our drive home from basketball practice. "It's the only sin that can't be forgiven because it's a lifestyle people choose." That was a common fundamentalist teaching—that being gay was an unforgivable sin because it was ever-present rather than a moment of sin (like theft or murder) that could be redeemed through repentance. When we went to watch women's basketball games at the local community college, my mom paid close attention to the women with short haircuts: "Julie, look at all those dykes wearing sweater-vests. I think that's how they signal to each other that they're gay—they wear sweater-vests!"

I made mental notes when these conversations came up: *Don't wear sweater-vests*, I thought to myself. *Don't be gay.*

My family moved to a suburb of Dallas right before I started high school, and my mom let me choose whether to go to school or keep homeschooling. That was an easy decision: I was going to public school. Even though I knew I'd be way behind from my childhood of no-schooling, I wanted to earn a college basketball scholarship. I enrolled at the local high school shortly after we moved, and that's where I met Sarah Turner, the first person I came out to—the woman I would eventually betray.

No one at my high school was more revered than Turner. A coach and beloved history teacher, she said "shit" around students, and in the days when teachers still hugged students, she gave us the kind of hugs that warmed us up from head to toe. She saw the best in us, from the football stars to the theater kids to the freaks and failures. More than anyone else in our school, she had the power to call forth tenderness from students with rough edges and courage from those of us who were insecure.

Turner was also a lesbian. When I was in high school, it was illegal to have gay sex, so LGBTQ teachers and coaches didn't come out. They told us they were gay through haircuts and button-up shirts. Occasionally, they told us through framed pictures of people they loved, proudly displayed on their desks in tiny acts of tender defiance. Turner didn't have to say she was a lesbian for everyone to know it, and for the most part, people didn't care. She was too adored for her sexuality to ruin her reputation.

I got to know Turner because I developed a close friendship with the star of our girls' soccer team during the spring of my freshman year. Erin was an all-American soccer player, and I was her biggest fan. I was in the stands cheering her on at every game, and every afternoon, I was spooning with her in her bed.

My mom quickly let me know she suspected Erin was a lesbian and that she was preying on me. The truth was more complicated than that, but my mom wasn't wrong that something gay was happening between us. I was enamored with Erin. I knew which hallways she took between classes, and I planned my route to intersect with hers. I never missed a soccer game. In my free time, I had one goal: to get to Erin's house so I could lie in bed next to her, drape my hand over her stomach, press my nose against her neck, and breathe in her scent. I don't know how she felt about me. Was she straight and simply liked the affection? Was she questioning her own sexuality but too scared to say it? Did she just like the attention? Whatever our relationship meant to her, it was a revelation for me.

My mom forbade me from seeing or speaking to Erin, even in the hallways at school. In my first real act of self-assertion, I started lying. By this point, my mom had ingested two decades of fundamentalist teaching that said gay people were an abomination, AIDS was God's judgment on "deviant homosexuals," and queer people were out to abuse children and destroy the family. She went into overdrive to protect me from the perceived lesbian influences in my life, behaving in ways I never saw her engage with my brothers.

She took to stalking me around town, cruising by the YMCA if I said I was going to work out and showing up at Erin's doorstep unannounced. She gave me my first cell phone and kept tabs on the call log; she put a tracker on our computer that gave her access to my emails. She even became a substitute teacher at my high school to monitor my behavior between classes. My mom's obsessive response to our friendship exacerbated my sense of longing for Erin; I needed the comfort and security of our relationship even more as my mom became unhinged.

I lived in a state of turmoil throughout my sophomore year, as Erin and I grew closer and my mom's controlling behavior drove me further away from her. Whenever I walked through the front door of our house, I never knew if my mom would be warm or hysterical. Each day, on my way home, I ran through a list of the worst things she could have discovered about me that day, but I never could anticipate the source of her despair: maybe she snooped through my old journals that morning and read a sentence out of context that set her off. Or maybe she stumbled upon a childhood photo of mine, and she was overcome with grief that the sweet little girl in the picture grew up to become a cold and emotionally withdrawn teenager who lied to be around a presumed lesbian. And I *was* emotionally withdrawn; it was the only way I knew to cope with her outbursts. The only moments when I felt safe were when I allowed myself to float away to a calm, quiet place where no one assumed the worst about me or interrogated me—or when I was near Erin.

"We have to talk to Turner," Erin concluded one day after school.

We huddled together in the women's locker room out in the field house, where we hoped my mom wouldn't find us.

"Turner will be able to help us—I just know it. Will you please talk to her, Julie?"

I promised I would, even though I knew there was nothing she could do.

Turner agreed to meet with me in her office one afternoon, and I emotionally unloaded. I told her all about my friendship with Erin. I talked about my Evangelical upbringing and my inability to resolve the tension I felt between my mom's rules and my longing for intimacy with Erin.

"Are you a lesbian?" Turner gently asked when I finally took a breath.

My chest tightened, and I stared at her desk for what felt like a whole minute of silence.

"I think so," I whispered.

"And are you in love with Erin?"

"I don't know."

Turner offered to help me navigate my confusion. She said, "I have a book I can loan you called *Holy Homosexuals*, and it might help you work through some of your questions. If you're up for it, I can let you into my office every day after school, and you can come read it here, so your mom doesn't find it at home. How does that sound?"

Turner's office became a haven for me in a tumultuous season of life. There was only one openly gay kid at my school and few queer adults on TV shows or in the media. When I finally connected with someone who was mostly out and relatable—a role model who looked and felt like me—I latched onto her. I wanted to be with Erin, but I wanted to be like Turner, and I took to studying her in invasive ways. I asked her where she went to church and then visited that church. I dug for information about her personal life from mutual friends. When I found out when and where she walked her two rescue dogs, I rerouted my jogging path to cross hers. I believe I even showed up at her house one day, unannounced, and she appropriately but gently said that whatever I needed to talk about would need to wait until the next day at school. Who knows, though? I could've dreamed up that encounter, so rich was my fantasy life about an intimate mentoring relationship with Turner.

3

I came out to my mom on Valentine's Day of my junior year of high school. Earlier that day, my assistant principal, Ms. Jackson, called my mom from school to tell her I was suspended for the rest of the week. My offense? The suspension slip read "Urinating on the classroom floor."

My chemistry teacher, Ms. Davis, refused to let anyone use the restroom during class. "That's what your hall-passing period is for," she snapped when we begged her to let us relieve ourselves. "If you choose to spend your hall-passing period talking and flirting, that's your prerogative!"

We resented Ms. Davis for her antibathroom policy. Every afternoon when we huddled around lab tables, we schemed ways to beat Ms. Davis at the bathroom game. "I'm going to tell her I'm on my period and that I'm bleeding through my tampon," my friend Jenna said one afternoon. As others weighed in on that suggestion, I got an idea: "Well, if someone has to use the restroom, and they're forbidden access to the toilets, then there's only one natural outcome of that decision." Everyone within earshot turned toward me. "Look, it wouldn't be my decision to have to go in my pants. It would be Ms. Davis's, for refusing to let me go." My classmates were giddy about my plan.

The next day, I intentionally wore shorts and drank plenty of Gatorade throughout the day. By the time I got to Ms. Davis's class, my need to go was urgent. Roughly fifteen minutes into her lecture, I raised my hand: "Excuse me, Ms. Davis, may I please go use the restroom?" She launched into the predictable hall-passing-period speech, so I got up and walked toward the door. "Please, Ms. Davis, it's an emergency!"

"Get in your seat!" Ms. Davis cried out.

"Oh my G—I'm going . . ." I said, looking down at the floor. Ms. Davis saw the pee running down my leg, pooling under my feet.

"Get out of here!" she screamed. "Run!"

I took off running, out of the classroom, down the hallway, into the restroom, and the entire way, I could not stop my bladder's impulse. After I made it to the restroom, I went to the women's locker room to shower and change clothes. When I returned to class, I was proud to have won the bathroom war with Ms. Davis.

My high from the victory came to an abrupt halt when Ms. Jackson, the assistant principal, met me at the door right after class. "Get in my office," she whisper-threatened. She called my mom on speakerphone and made me tell her what I had done. This pee incident was the third or fourth prank I had pulled in a matter of months. In addition to granting myself off-campus lunches (a privilege only seniors were given), I had blown up a condom and thrown it off the main bridge on the second floor of our school during student rush hour. I hung off that same bridge another afternoon, as if I might jump, just to get attention. It was a desperate attempt to communicate that I was scared and hurting.

Ms. Jackson said that if I had one more infraction, I would spend the rest of the year in Compass, our community's alternative school.

When I left school that afternoon, I called a woman who had recently become a mentor. Her name was Mrs. Jarvis, and she was a substitute teacher who also happened to be a sweet southern Baptist with a big heart and a surprising capacity for complexity. She took me to her son's hockey practice the first time we hung out, and within a few weeks of knowing her, I told her all about the challenges I faced.

"Jules, I think you should tell your mom what's going on," she said to me on the phone as I walked through my school's parking lot.

"Honestly, she probably already knows," she continued. "And if it catches her by surprise and she tells you to leave, then you can come stay at our house."

My mom would need some sort of explanation for my pee stunt, so it wasn't the worst time to come out. I also agreed with Mrs. Jarvis that my mom likely knew. Besides, moving into the Jarvises' sounded awesome. I figured I had nothing to lose.

When I walked through the front door of my house that day, my mom was sitting on a love seat in the living room with a worn Bible open on her lap. Her eyes were red and swollen.

"What's going on with you, Julie?" Her voice cracked.

I stared at the off-white carpet on the floor and opened my mouth to speak before I had decided how to position what I was going to tell her.

"Well, I've been wanting to talk to you about something for a while. I don't really know how to say it. I guess I've thought for a long time that I might be gay, or bisexual, or something. I don't know. I'm attracted to other girls, and I can't do anything about it. I don't really know what to say. I'm sorry."

She leapt up from the love seat and threw herself down next to me. She wrapped her arms around me and wailed, rocking me back and forth. I wanted to break out of her arms and breathe. I needed space. But at that time, I didn't think my needs were allowed to be as important as my mother's. So I let her hold me. I let her tears wet my cheek as she mourned the death of the daughter who lived in her imagination.

"I'm sorry, Mom," I said after a minute. "I'm so sorry."

I escaped to my bedroom as quickly as I could and waited for my dad to get home. I hadn't thought much about how he might respond, but I knew his presence would relieve some of the tension in the house. After an hour or two, I heard a knock at the door.

"I've got to run to the store to pick up some things for dinner," my dad said. "Why don't you come with me?"

He wasted no time once we got in his car. He pulled away from the curb, turned down the radio, and gently patted my knee as he started to speak.

"Mom says you told her you're gay."

"Yeah, I think so," I said, surprised that he just said "gay"— not bisexual, or confused, or struggling with my sexuality.

"Now, you listen to me," he said with an intensity I rarely heard in his voice. "Whatever happens, you remember your daddy loves you no matter what."

"Okay, thanks," I said.

"Do you understand me?" He started again, speaking slowly, careful to articulate each word. "Your daddy loves you *no matter what*. Don't ever forget it."

He knocked his fist against my knee.

"Don't you ever forget it."

I was too withdrawn to match his vulnerability then, but his words made a lasting impression. My dad's words conveyed a sense of impending doom, as if one of us was about to embark on a treacherous journey from which we might not return. He spoke with a sense of urgency, his words both comforting and foreboding. My parents loved me—that was clear from both of their responses. What was unclear was how they were going to channel that love when it came to the next steps.

The next day, my mom dropped me off at my brother's house. Michael was eight years older than me, and he had done everything he was supposed to do: he graduated from Texas A&M University a year early with a degree in finance, got married at twenty-one to a girl he met working at a Christian camp, attended a conservative Evangelical church several times a week, and voted Republican. Based on how he spoke, it was clear: there was right and there was wrong. You did what was right. It was simple.

We sat on the curb outside his apartment so we could have some privacy while his wife did chores inside. I only remember one thing he said: "Well, Julie, I hope you don't choose to be gay, because I want you to be able to come around my kids as they grow up."

Bringing my knees into my chest, I wrapped my arms around my legs and rested my chin on my knees, making myself as small as possible as I sat with his words. "That makes sense," I said, looking down at the ground.

Meanwhile, my mom was back home, calling everyone who might be able to help her find a biblical answer to the problem. Within days, she learned there were others like me. She heard about people who experienced same-sex attractions and, through the power of the gospel, changed.

A few days later, my mom pulled me out of school early to meet with a minister who she heard could help me become straight.

We got lost on our way to meet him. For twenty or thirty minutes, we took U-turns and wrong turns, all within a mile of our destination.

"We already turned down this street," I said at one point, trying to help her navigate.

"Have a little grace for me, Julie!" She was crying again. "This isn't easy for me, okay! This isn't what I envisioned for my baby girl."

We pulled into the parking lot, late. That morning, with the meeting in mind, I chose to wear my varsity letter jacket, baggy jeans, and sneakers. This pastor needed to understand that I was not feminine. I was not interested in trying to appear to be anyone other than my lesbian self.

My mom and I hurried into the office building where First Baptist Church of Arlington rented space. We gave our names to a receptionist and waited to speak with the minister who my mom believed would save me.

o o o

"You must be Julie." A stocky, middle-aged man with black hair and wire-rimmed glasses stretched his hand out to shake mine. "Ricky Chelette. I'm the singles minister here at First Baptist, and I meet with young people like you in my free time."

He shook my mom's hand and asked us both to sign some papers before inviting me to join him in the conference room next door. "Connie, there's a coffee shop across the street if you want to hang out there while we talk."

My mom looked alarmed at the thought of me meeting with Ricky without her.

"We'll be done in about two hours if you want to come back then."

Within the first few minutes, I learned that Ricky, who would later become the executive director of an ex-gay organization called Living Hope Ministries, was himself attracted to men.

"I struggle with same-sex attractions," he admitted up front. "But God has been so faithful to me. I'm happily married to a gorgeous woman named Merlinda. She's an ICU nurse. She's got bright-green eyes and hair that's as red as a fire truck, and I'm madly in love with her."

I learned that they had two dogs, a southern chic home, and a kitchen table that seated twelve people. They believed it was their responsibility to welcome people who weren't wanted elsewhere.

Ricky used dry-erase markers on the glass tabletop in the conference room to illustrate his theory about why people experience same-sex attractions. The gist of his theory was that we hadn't connected with our same-sex parents the way we were supposed to in childhood, and our desire for intimacy with our same-sex parent was sexualized at puberty.

"We're drawn to that which is mysterious," Ricky said. "For children who develop normally, they connect deeply with their same-sex parent, and their opposite-sex parent is mysterious; they're different. When a boy who develops normally hits puberty, the intrigue he felt about his mother is eroticized, and he develops normal, healthy attractions to other girls. For those of us who experience same-sex attractions, the opposite happens. The good news is that if we develop healthy relationships with people of the same gender now, we can demystify them and, over time, start to feel desire for the opposite sex."

Then he launched into a neurological explanation of how exactly our attractions change. He sketched objects that looked like wiry starfish on the glass table as he continued.

"These little things here are called neurons. Our brains have billions of these neurons, and every time you orgasm, it creates a synaptic connection that associates whatever was in your brain with pleasure. Orgasms obviously feel really good! So your brain makes a positive association with the object you were thinking about when you orgasmed. Over time, you've created a pathway in your brain that's reinforced thousands of times through things like porn, masturbation, and acting out with another person—which can almost seal your fate."

"Are you still with me?" he asked, looking up from the table.

"Um, I think so."

"Okay, because now we're getting to the good news: these synaptic connections work both ways. Just like we can sort of program ourselves to be attracted to the same gender by reinforcing the pleasure pathways in our brains when we think about people of the same sex, we can literally rewire our brains to feel that same desire for the opposite sex over time. Isn't God amazing?"

It was a lot to take in. I leaned forward and set my elbow on the table, resting my chin in my hand with my fingers curled over my mouth. The drawings were a convenient distraction, so I didn't have to hold eye contact with Ricky.

"How do you explain people who have great relationships with their same-sex parent and still end up gay?" I looked at the drawing as I asked.

"Ah, you're getting ahead of me. Almost every struggler I've met over the years tells me I've just drawn their whole entire life out when they see this diagram," he said as he colored clothes onto his stick-figure drawings. That's how he referred to queer people—*strugglers*.

I thought about whether I could locate my story in his drawing.

"But there's one wild card," Ricky continued. "Sexual abuse. God knew the power of sex when he created us. In God's original plan, we wait until we're married and then we only have sex with one person in that sacred union for the rest of our lives. When a child is exposed to sex, it blows everything up, and the brokenness comes out in all kinds of ways, including same-sex attractions."

According to Ricky, if you had a great relationship with both of your parents and you told him you weren't sexually abused, then you were likely lying to yourself about your so-called great relationship with your parents or you had buried your memories of sexual abuse. Every "struggler" fit into this diagram.

His argument implied that I was not actually gay. I was a straight person who misfired from time to time.

"Well, how does all this sit with you?" he finally asked.

"Honestly, I think this is bullshit," I said firmly, slouching back into my chair. "I'm gay. I'm just gay. And I'm totally cool with it. I just need everyone else in my life to be okay with it."

I had planned on having that kind of response to him prior to even meeting him—I simply wasn't interested in the ministry he offered. But after hearing his spiel, I quietly wondered if he might be right about some of the psychology behind my attractions. After all, my relationship with my mom *was* unhealthy. I felt closer to my dad and brothers, and I'd always been "one of the guys." Plus, my "education" as a homeschooler didn't include science, so I spent all of high school trying to catch up and still didn't understand the basics. His explanation of how we end up gay made sense to my teenage brain.

The next week, I was taken back to Ricky's office. I didn't have any good options. My mom had been frantic since I came out, and my dad appeared to be doing what he had always done: yielding to my mom's wishes. I still had another year and a half in my parents' home. I needed someone who understood what it was like to feel like a foreigner in their home and faith community, even if they identified as "same-sex attracted" and believed gay love was sinful.

I didn't have access to any wise gay Christian elders who, by their existence, communicated to me that you could tell the truth about yourself and have a positive future. At the age of sixteen, I had two options: leave my home and the only life I had ever known or try to become straight.

Over the next few months, Ricky tried to create a safe place for me to work through my baggage. He was an adult who was interested in my childhood, my questions, my crushes at school, and my dreams for the future. I felt like Ricky saw me. He didn't see the version of myself I felt I was supposed to be in order for people to accept me; he saw my grief and cynicism and the soft heart beneath it all. More important, my mom seemed optimistic when I met with Ricky. Living Hope was a stabilizing force in our family. As long as I was trying to change, we were okay.

o o o

"I need to see everyone in the living room. We're having a family meeting right now." My mom stood in the hallway outside of my bedroom, calling out to me, Kenny, and my dad in a stern and somber tone. Kenny and I emerged from our bedrooms at the same time, exchanging raised-eyebrow looks, as if to say, "What could it be this time?"

My mom sat down in her seat, which was a cushion on the blue-and-white plaid love seat, next to a stack of papers, bills, torn envelopes, and Christian books. She thumbed through some loose pages on her lap as the rest of us settled into our seats. I took the farthest seat in the room from my mom on the couch. Kenny sat next to me, and my dad settled into his usual rocking chair, with his legs crossed at the knee, directly across the room from my mom.

"Kenny and I came home from the Barnabas Retreat on a real spiritual high," my mom began. "I can't remember the last time I felt so hopeful, like we had turned a corner and God was really moving. They told us, right before we left, to be prepared for a spiritual attack because these mountaintop moments are always the times when Satan feels most threatened by us. I just didn't expect the attack to come so soon."

My breath quickened as my mind raced through reasons I could be responsible for her downward emotional spiral.

"I got on the computer to look up some resources they recommended at the retreat, and I don't even know how, but the internet history came up on the screen. I wasn't even looking for it."

I struggled to swallow.

"I am completely shocked by what I found," she said, eyes wide, as she looked through her reading glasses at the pages in her hands. "www.GirlOnGirlAction.com." Her voice cracked as she read. "www.HotGirls69.com . . ."

"Okay, Mom, we get it," Kenny interrupted. "Julie looked at porn."

"www.LesbiansGoneWild.com, www.BadGirlsXXX .com . . ." She let out a whimper.

"Do you really need to read through the whole list of sites she looked at?" Kenny asked.

My face heated up as I stared at the books and coasters on the coffee table in front of me. My thoughts raced from explanations to panic.

"Do you want to explain this, Julie?" My mom took off her glasses and leaned back in her seat, glaring at me from across the room.

"I was just curious to see what was out there," I said, waving my hand at nothing. "It was the first time I've looked at anything like that. I don't know, I wanted to know what kinds of things people do."

"But it's all *lesbian* porn!" she cried.

"Yeah," Kenny piped up. "Julie's into girls, which means her sexual falls are gonna involve women."

My mom burst into tears. My dad gently patted his hair, sitting in the rocking chair next to me.

"Did this really need to be a family meeting?" Kenny asked. "Couldn't you have just talked to Julie about this privately?"

I stared at the unlit fireplace across the room. Kenny slumped deeper into the couch. My dad remained silent.

"I'm really sorry," I said after a few moments of silence. "I feel really bad that I ruined your awesome weekend."

I don't remember how the meeting ended because I zoned out midway through it. What else could I do with the reminder that I was a source of anguish to the only person I wanted to please? The weight of my mom's disappointment was too great a burden to bear. I felt helpless, embarrassed, incapable of being the kind of daughter who would make my mom happy.

o o o

My mom was eager to give God the credit when we realized my club basketball team had a tournament in Orlando that ended the day before Exodus International's annual conference started in, of all places, Orlando. "This is such a God thing!" she marveled.

Exodus was the largest organization in the world that advertised "freedom from homosexuality" through a relationship with Jesus. They were a hub that connected smaller ministries like Living Hope all over the world, and every summer, their national conferences drew thousands of people looking for hope and community. These conferences were like church camp for people who struggled with same-sex attractions. For one week out of the year, no one had to hide the thing that always made them feel different and ashamed. When we looked around the auditorium at all the clean-cut men and women in button-up shirts and wide-legged jeans, it was one of the rare moments when we knew we weren't alone.

It was July of 2003, the summer before my senior year in high school, and I was seventeen years old. Minors weren't allowed to attend Exodus conferences unless they were accompanied by their parents, but Ricky was taking a group and offered to look out for me.

After my tournament ended, my mom and I drove to a hotel, where we were supposed to meet some of the twenty-somethings from Living Hope, who would escort me to the conference safely. I had interacted with some of these new friends through the online forums Ricky moderated. There were more than five thousand people on Living Hope's message boards from more than seventy-five different countries. The youth forum, which included everyone under twenty-seven years old, had several hundred active members. We were forbidden from sharing personal information for fear that we might connect with each other offline and have sex, so we only knew each other's first names. We typed hundreds of pages about our families and sexual fantasies—for accountability, we were encouraged to tell each other when we masturbated—but we didn't know each other's last names. Those who were caught sharing identifying information about themselves were kicked off the forums and disconnected from the community. The only exception to the no-contact rule was at ex-gay conferences where Ricky chaperoned.

At a Red Roof Inn somewhere in the shadows of Disney World, my mom and I knocked on the door of a room where I would meet some of these online strangers face-to-face. I was most excited to meet Jason. Jason was working on the first of what would become two doctorate degrees. He was the opinionated, compassionate, articulate son of a Black preacher, and his presence was felt even when he was silent. Jason quickly became a big brother to me and, at every point in my journey, he was a few steps ahead of me with a hand reaching back, waving me onward. After I met Jason, an Egyptian film student named Mark and a gamer named Mel returned from a day of exploring. They bought quirky gifts for everyone in the room, so my anxious mom left that night with a large, uncooked corn on the cob, which only exacerbated her anxiety.

"I'm just not comfortable leaving my baby girl in a dingy hotel room with a bunch of strangers who struggle with homosexuality," she said through tears as I walked her out to the rental car. "Don't they seem weird to you?"

"It'll be fine," I reassured her. "We're going to meet up with the rest of the group at the conference tonight, and I'll be with Ricky the rest of the time."

I grabbed my bags and hugged her, then headed back to the room to hang out with my new friends.

At the age of seventeen, I thought the people in our Living Hope group were as cool as humans came. A guy named Seth had just returned from nine months in Thailand. Casey from the Northeast had spikey blond hair with multiple piercings. Jake was a football coach from the West Coast, and James was a fashion-forward sweetie pie from Georgia. Most of my new friends had already graduated from college, so not only were they the first group of not-straights I had ever been around, but they were infinitely cooler than everyone my age.

I was surprised to find that, like Ricky, most of the leaders of the other ex-gay ministries at Exodus also "struggled" with same-sex attractions. There were hundreds of leaders and therapists doing the same work Ricky was doing in states across the country, and I can count on one hand the ones who said they had never struggled with homosexuality.

For most of the week, I kept my guard up: I sat stoically during the peppy worship songs and made fun of everyone who cheerfully proclaimed hope for "healing." I mocked the teachers of the "embracing your true femininity" workshop. It was at that Exodus conference that I smoked my first cigarette, and I said "fuck" as often and loudly as possible. Who I was, I didn't know, but I was not about that shit.

And yet, on the final night, as the worship band played, I found myself weeping. The closing keynote speaker had just made us howl with laughter and choke up with heart-wrenching stories. All the speakers said they were happier now than they had been in the days when they embraced their same-sex desires and lived as openly gay people. Sure, they still struggled with same-sex attractions, these heterosexually married men said, but those attractions were like flies they had to swat away from time to time. They had Jesus now. They weren't at war with themselves. They had undivided hearts.

I wanted an undivided heart. I wanted a relationship with Jesus. And I wanted to share in the community of Christians, especially the Christians I met that week. It seemed as if only one choice had to be made and a whole world would open up to me: a world where my parents and Ricky would be proud of me, where God would be pleased with me, and where these new friends would become my family. In a wooden pew at Fourth Presbyterian Church in Orlando, after forty-five minutes of crying while the band played and Ricky held me in a warm embrace, I said yes to Jesus again that night, just like I had on my mom's bathroom floor a decade earlier. I said no to my flesh, no to my sexuality.

When I boarded a plane to go back home, I was returning as a senior in high school who was sold out for Jesus.

4

The Exodus conference was in July of 2003, and by August, my mom and Ricky decided I would transfer from my high school, a public school with more than two thousand students, to a Christian school with a graduating class of thirteen students for my senior year. As a freshman, I had started on the varsity basketball team and was recruited to play at the college level with some of the best programs in the country. I was an athlete who had peaked in her freshman year, so top-tier universities weren't open to me, but full-ride scholarships to smaller schools were on the table. I feared that transferring to a tiny Evangelical school might jeopardize my chances of signing with a good university.

That didn't matter, my mom said, because I would be going to a Christian college.

"Lesbians are everywhere in sports at secular colleges, and your relationship with Jesus is more important than a basketball scholarship!"

Not only would I be transferring to an Evangelical school to get away from the evil influences at public school, but I would also be scheduling an appointment with my old school district's superintendent to register my concerns about Turner, the only gay mentor I had ever had.

Turner's name came up often in my conversations with Ricky, and with my mom's influence, we began to rewrite the story of my relationship with Turner. She had recruited me. She had identified in me some traits that reminded her of other lesbians (my athleticism and tomboyish tendencies), and she targeted me. She took my question marks and made them periods, convincing me I was a lesbian when I, in my innocence, would not have considered it. Her superiors needed to be informed about what she was doing to stop her from bringing her agenda into the lives of children in our community. Otherwise, she would continue preying upon other students like me.

My mom scheduled meetings with Ms. Jackson, my assistant principal, and Mr. Hicks, my guidance counselor. She laid out the case against Turner, and Ms. Jackson was eager to conspire against her lesbian colleague. She agreed that, yes, Turner had been incredibly inappropriate in her interactions with me, and she needed to be held accountable. We needed to schedule an appointment with the superintendent, and Ms. Jackson would be happy to offer her testimony in support, since she had seen me reading in Turner's office after school on multiple occasions. My mom promptly set the appointment, and it was decided that Ricky would accompany me to meet with the superintendent.

My chest tightened every time I thought about turning on Turner. She had been the one adult in my life who had truly seen me and empathized with me. She tried to give me the gift of affirmation and belonging that she knew no one else in a conservative Christian community would offer me as a lesbian. She took a risk when she became my advocate, informing me on days when my mom was a substitute at my school and opening up her office to me as a safe place to read books I couldn't take home. Despite my needy efforts to pry into her life, she had compassion for me. At a time and in a community where it still wasn't safe for an adult to be out in the school system, she was vulnerable with me in an effort to help me. And I was going to turn her in.

Ricky and I met each other outside of the superintendent's office. He pulled me in close to him with a side hug and assured me again that I was doing the right thing. He said I was brave. We walked into the office, I told the superintendent about my relationship with Turner, and I offered up the narrative of recruitment we had rehearsed. I left the superintendent's office with a dry throat, a tight chest, and an empty feeling in my gut. But when I walked through the door of my house that afternoon, all was calm. We were on the same team now. There would be no need for fighting or crying or spying. I was committed to Living Hope, sold out to the process of becoming straight. All the evil influences had been removed from my life, and we were okay.

To this day, I feel ashamed of myself for betraying Turner.

In November of my senior year in high school, three months after that first Exodus conference, Ricky asked me to give my ex-gay testimony at Living Hope's donor banquet.

"I'm not sure I'm ready," I wondered aloud. "I don't know what my story is at this point."

He would help with that, he reassured me. What was important was my willingness to allow God's glory to shine through me as I spoke of God's healing work in my life.

In Evangelical communities, testimonies have a pretty standard structure: the speaker lived in darkness for much of their life (the more sensational, the better). Then, after a period of drug addiction or sex work or a bout with a disruptive venereal disease, the person realized they were helpless and desperate for a savior. They then have a spiritual encounter and decide to give their life to Jesus. This commitment is commonly enacted by walking to the altar at the close of a church service or by raising their hand when a pastor asks if anyone would like to accept Jesus as their Lord and Savior right then. They say a prayer of surrender, and then everything changes. God's Holy Spirit fills them and infuses their life with purpose. They're flooded with an unexplainable sense of peace. There is a clear "before" and "after" that is split directly in half by the moment of their conversion to Christianity.

Ricky helped me craft my speech, with all of the flair of the typical Evangelical testimony: I had been living in darkness (which meant I had a confusing friendship with Erin and secretly attended a queer church on two occasions). I was wrapped up in the gay lifestyle until my mom dragged me, kicking and screaming, to meet with Ricky. After six months of resisting God's love, poured out to me through Ricky, I finally gave in and surrendered my life to Jesus. Then, at the age of seventeen, I was a new creation, filled with hope and compassion.

The standard ex-gay testimony had its own twist, taking the Evangelical testimony a step further by incorporating reparative therapy talking points into the story. Almost every ex-gay testimony reflected widely discredited psychological theories: the speaker felt distant from their same-sex parent, overidentified with their opposite-sex parent, sometimes experienced sexual abuse, and found themselves with same-sex attractions when puberty hit. They usually spent some time living in "sexual sin" (the racier, the better) until they gave their life to Jesus. Ricky coached me on how to structure my testimony, which included the narrative about Turner pushing lesbianism upon me. It played right into the fears of conservative audience members, who saw me as an innocent victim of the secular gay agenda.

My speech was so well received that, as a teenager, I was invited to become a regular whenever Ricky spoke at events around the city. When he taught at churches or Christian schools about why people became gay and how God could heal them, I was invited along to share my story before his presentation. I incorporated Ricky's key points into my testimony to serve as a model illustration of how a kid could end up struggling with homosexuality. But God, I reassured them, (mainly through Living Hope!) wouldn't let me out of his grip.

I didn't make any money from those talks, but my compensation was better than cash: I got to ride to every event in the passenger seat of Ricky's dark-green Mercedes Benz. We often drove an hour each way and shared a meal afterward, which meant I received three to four hours of attention every time we spoke together. We talked about our weeks and told stories about our pasts. We debriefed the event on the drive home, when Ricky highlighted the powerful moments in my testimony, with occasional pointers about how I could improve. We laughed at inside jokes, wrestled with theological questions, and sometimes sat in comfortable silence together. Of all the people Ricky could've chosen to mentor so closely, I often marveled to myself, he chose me.

I didn't know then that saying yes to Ricky's request for me to join him as a speaker meant that I would be processing unresolved questions about my faith and sexuality on a public stage. The human brain is still developing well into our midtwenties. I had only received four years of real education at that point, and I still had college ahead of me. I had not yet seen the consequences of ex-gay teaching on my vulnerable friends. I couldn't have known that Exodus International would ask me to join their speaking team and that I would essentially grow up in the national spotlight in one of our country's most heated debates. I was seventeen years old. I only wanted to please my parents.

○　○　○

Every Thursday evening at First Baptist Church of Arlington, more than a hundred people who struggled with same-sex attractions strolled into a room where only Ricky knew their last name. Living Hope wasn't the kind of place you could show up unannounced; you went through an intake interview with Ricky or Amber, the women's director, before you were approved to attend the support group. And like the online forum, contact with members outside of the group context was strictly forbidden. We weren't allowed to share our last names, contact information, or any identifying information, such as where we went to church or school. "We are not going to be an underground dating site for strugglers," Ricky would say. "We're here to help people find healing."

For the first ten or fifteen minutes of a given gathering, we hugged in the hallways and caught up about our weeks. Twentysomethings made up about half the group most weeks, and there were always more men than women. As we greeted each other, we checked out the new people and stole glances at crushes. The earnest ones quickly averted their eyes; the rest of us held gazes and felt a rebellious rush. Even Ricky frequently

commented on guys in the ministry he thought were "hot."
("I bet he's hung like a horse," I once heard him say about a
tall guy in the young men's group.)

Every week, we were reminded that we weren't gay. The
terms *gay* and *lesbian* were sinful identities people chose to use
when they defined themselves by their sexuality rather than
their identity in Christ. We were "strugglers." We were over-
comers! We were children of God.

The first half of group meetings felt like any other church
gathering: we began by singing a few worship songs together
to the tune of a wooden piano played by a small-group leader.
After worship, Ricky taught for about forty-five minutes. He
usually preached his way straight through books of the Bible,
so his sermons were based on the verses that came up on a
given week rather than a topic he chose. Whatever the Scripture
for that week, though, his talks looped back around to themes
of sexual immorality, the dangers of the flesh, and the need
to die to ourselves so we could live for Christ.

What kept people like me coming back was that he often
spoke about grace too. We heard sermons about sexual immorality and brokenness all the time, and we were accustomed to
the sense of shame those talks induced. What we weren't used
to—what drew us back to Living Hope—was the possibility for
wholeness. Most of us came from families that didn't accept
us, and many of us worked for Christian employers that would
fire us if they knew we weren't straight. We were used to feeling like we carried a contagious disease. We weren't used to a
community that offered us hope.

After the sermon, we split up into small groups—that's
where the conversations got juicy. Four groups met each week:
parents of queer kids, women, adult men, and young men,

which included all the guys under the age of twenty-seven. Each group had a facilitator, and everyone got a chance to share about their week. The small group leader engaged with each member individually, the way a therapist would interact with a client—with active listening, probing questions, encouragement, accountability, and advice. Crosstalk between group members was forbidden.

Ricky led the youth group, and that group began with each of the twenty to thirty young men going around in a circle and giving a number, one through ten, to rate their week. Ten meant you had anal sex that week. Nine was oral sex. Eight indicated that you made out with another man and likely fondled each other. Porn put you at a five or a six (depending on whether a webcam was involved), and masturbation made you a two or three (depending on how compulsive it was and who you fantasized about). If you were a one, then your week was virtually perfect, sexually speaking. The most time was allotted for the higher numbers, so the tens went first, and on down the line.

Small group time was when we confessed our sexual failures or admitted to reaching out to an ex. We were to cut off all contact with former lovers, even if we hadn't crossed physical boundaries. We were to avoid anything that might intensify our identification with the queer parts of ourselves, which could include things like listening to queer musicians or watching films that featured LGBTQ characters. At some point, I had to confess to my small group at Living Hope that I had been hiding DVDs of *The L Word* underneath my mattress in my room. *The L Word* was the first TV series with an entire cast of queer women. I watched the show wide-eyed and short of breath because it was exhilarating to see so many lesbians living their everyday lives: cooking dinner together at the end of a long day, making coffee on a lazy Saturday morning, navigating the complications of coming out in a world that didn't like queer women. For the first time, I was able to locate my experience in characters like me who faced similar challenges and survived. They made it. They were relatively well adjusted, and they weren't alone. In my circles, shows like *The L Word* were seen as propaganda that were manufactured to push a gay agenda that would exacerbate our struggles with same-sex attraction and cause us to lust. In my small group, I confessed that I had secretly been watching the show, and I recommitted myself to the healing process.

If we misbehaved during the week, we analyzed why exactly we had done it in our small groups. With the help of our leaders, we often made connections between an upsetting conversation with a parent and a fall to masturbation later that day. Or maybe a boss belittled us and made us feel insecure—that's why we reached out to our old crush that week. Our moral failures could've been due to something as simple as a same-sex friend ignoring our texts; there was always a psychological reason for our surge of same-sex desire.

After the small groups let out, we gathered outside on the south side of the church to socialize. All the young people went to TGI Fridays after group, chaperoned by Ricky and Amber. For one night each week, we were with peers who knew the anguish we faced each night, the shame we felt around our families, the self-hatred we experienced every time we felt our bodies respond to a crush.

Despite the ways Living Hope reinforced the toxic messages that contributed to our communities' hostility toward queer people, the ministry was gentler toward us than most Christians were at that time, even kinder than much of the broader culture. It was illegal for people in Texas to have gay sex in the privacy of their own homes. Several of the older men in the ministry were outed to their wives and children because they were arrested in sting operations when they had sex with other men. LGBTQ people were rarely featured in mainstream films or TV shows. We were not celebrated for coming out in our schools. We were "dykes" and "faggots" and targets for harassment. There was no national Pride month. There were no rainbow Coke cans. We only had our secrets, our shame, and each other.

The first time I burned myself, I was sitting on a curb outside of the church after a Living Hope meeting. This was usually one of the more joyful moments in our weeks, when we whispered about the new hotties and gossiped about the ones who made risqué confessions in small group. The boys wrapped me in their arms and joked about dating me because they didn't know how else to express their repressed sexuality. And yet, whether we discussed it openly or not, we were in pain.

I felt a heightened sense of despair on this particular Thursday night. As my cigarette burned low, without giving it much thought, I shoved the burning end of it into my shoulder and listened as the skin on my left arm sizzled.

"Oh my God, what are you doing?" my friend Daniel barked.

"I don't know," I mumbled as I observed the burn. "It just felt right."

Shortly after that night, I sat alone in my room, lost in a whirlwind of fear, agony, and self-loathing. That's when I remembered the cigarette burn and the wave of detachment that flowed through my body the moment the fire seared my skin. After scanning my room for metal objects that would heat under fire, I landed on a quarter. Clamping the quarter with tweezers, I plunged it into the flame of a lighter, my heart rate rising as the coin heated up. I inhaled, flexed my left arm, and pressed the quarter deep into my flesh until the skin broke and the pain numbed.

I repeated the process at least twenty times that afternoon, searing straight lines into my shoulder, each a few inches wide. I remember glaring into a small round mirror that sat on my desk and saying "fuck you" as the burns became numb. Every "you" in those moments was a Christian leader who told my parents not to accept their own daughter. It was the administration at my Evangelical school that made it impossible for me to tell the truth about myself and belong. But more than anyone else, the "fuck you" was directed at me.

That evening, the wounds were white. A few days later, many of them had turned black, and liquid oozed through my T-shirts when I was in class. For weeks, I engaged in a routine of applying Neosporin to the wounds every morning and evening. This ritual became a way to self-soothe, a means by which to experience a healing in my body that I had not obtained through Living Hope's support group, counseling with Ricky, or healing prayer. We were safe in those moments, me and my body. I could roll up my shirt sleeve, expose my wounds, and be met with tenderness and compassion.

In the years that followed, when the anguish became unbearable, I would return to this routine: burning straight lines into my shoulders and tending to the wounds to self-soothe. Once both shoulders were used up, I applied my homemade branding technique to places where previous scars existed, ripping through the skin again, causing more severe wounds than before.

I've heard depression described as anger turned inward. Perhaps that's what I was doing in my room all those years ago: I took the rage I felt about living in a body that couldn't be submitted into the kind of body it was supposed to be—a straight body, a feminine body, a good Christian body—and I lit it on fire.

5

I moved in with Ricky the summer after my sophomore year in college. The year leading up to the move had been a year of experimentation: I smoked pot with acquaintances and stayed out past my Christian college's curfew. I was put on probation for having a hookah. ("I'm very familiar with the hucka," my RD said when I asked her if she knew what it was.) I hooked up with a few girls I met on Myspace and a handful of guys I met out and about. After a sexual encounter with a regular from the coffee shop where I worked as a barista, Ricky concluded that only one thing could save me: total lockdown. He suggested I move in with him and his wife, Merlinda, for the summer. He would take my car keys, my computer, my cell phone—any device that would connect to the outside world. He would drive me to work every morning, where I would journal, study the Bible, and read Christian books until my shift in the afternoons. It was voluntary, of course, but it was the only way forward, as far as he could see. By that point, I could no longer distinguish between Ricky's suggestions and the voice of God.

"Julie, I have some bad news," Ricky said to me as I walked down the step from his kitchen to the living room, where we watched Fox News and HGTV in the dim light. "Your mom had a heart attack."

"*What*," I said, more as a statement than a question. I sat down on the dark-brown leather couch beside Ricky's chair and propped my feet up next to his on his footstool.

"I know. It's crazy. I just got off the phone with your dad. He said she's okay but that she had a heart attack this morning. They're doing tests on her now to try to figure out what happened."

"Did she take too many pills?" I asked, confused. "Isn't she too young to have a heart attack out of the blue?"

"There's no tellin' with her." His thick Louisiana accent came through as he shook his head side to side. "Why don't you get ready and we'll head up to the hospital."

In the tan leather back seat of Ricky's forest-green Mercedes, I thought about what I would say to my mom when we got to the hospital. She and I hadn't spoken much since I started lockdown at the beginning of the summer. I knew she was disappointed in me. She called me in tears after Ricky told her about our summer plans, especially when he said I was on the brink of destruction and that lockdown was a last-ditch effort to save me. She also indicated that she was jealous of my relationship with Ricky. "It's like he's your mom and dad all wrapped into one," she said to me a few months earlier, when she asked why I left my family's holiday celebrations early to spend the rest of the day at Ricky's, why I went antiquing with him and never wanted to shop with her, why I went to church with him and had lunch at his house every Sunday afternoon. Now I had moved in with him.

Nevertheless, she did not want a lesbian daughter, and if Ricky could save me, then she would consent to the program.

I walked into the hospital room with a sense of dread, not because I feared bad news but because I was always nervous to see my mom, always afraid I was in trouble. Then I saw her lying in the hospital bed, with IVs buried in the soft underside of her elbows and machines beeping beside her. In an instant, I moved from worry to an overwhelming sense of pity. My strong-willed mom, utterly helpless and alone.

"I'm so sorry, Mom," I said softly as I rubbed her foot at the end of the bed.

"Connie, how are you doing?" Ricky asked as Merlinda crowded in behind him. "We've been prayin' for you ever since we heard the news."

"Oh, I'm fine," she said with a scowl. She went on to tell us how it happened, how she didn't know she was having a heart attack at the time, how my dad called the ambulance just in case, since she seemed a little off. I was glad they still lived together. Even though I saw no tenderness between them, it was nice to know another human was around to call an ambulance.

"I'm just so sorry, Mom," I said again after she finished her story.

"What are you sorry about?" she snapped back.

"I don't know—it just makes me sad to see you in pain, hooked up to all these machines."

"Julie, the pain of this heart attack is nothing compared to the pain you've caused me," she said, her dark-brown eyes locked on mine.

I shifted my gaze to the sheets on her bed. "Well, I'm still sorry," I mumbled.

Ricky said something to fill the silence, and as he spoke, I felt a magnetic pull to him. It was rare for someone outside of my family to hear the casual ways my mother shamed me, the skillful ways she twisted things to make me feel responsible for her misery. Her rejection felt more bearable with Ricky nearby.

I wanted to melt into him, to feel him wrap me up in a warm embrace and pull my head into his chest.

After a few more minutes, I squeezed my mom's hand and told her I loved her, then followed Ricky and Merlinda outside of the hospital room to the back seat of their car that would take me to their home. The familiar smell of Ricky's car put me at ease, and I allowed myself to escape into the fantasy that Ricky was my father and Merlinda my mother.

Lockdown stretched through the end of summer, into the fall, until courses at my Baptist college started back up. Ricky reinstated some of my privileges: I needed my car for the half-hour commute to school, but I was not to use it to go anywhere other than work or school. He said he put a tracker on my computer that would alert him to any inappropriate behavior online, and while I wasn't convinced he actually did that, I got his point: I was being watched.

"Well, you know God sees everything, so it shouldn't matter if I get a report," he said when I pressed him.

When I moved out to be on my own for the rest of my time in college, I lived within a one-mile radius of Ricky's house or office. Every Thursday night, I was at Living Hope's support group. On Tuesday nights, I went to a healing prayer group. I went through three rounds of an inner-healing curriculum called Living Waters with Ricky, each time hoping it would heal me of my body's natural desire for love and affection. Ricky gave me a part-time job at Living Hope, so I spent free days at a small desk right outside his office, where I entered data and edited articles for the monthly newsletter.

I also continued to give my testimony whenever Ricky spoke, despite my growing concerns about the way my story functioned. Throughout most of my time in high school and college, I didn't understand how the details of a life can be rearranged and interpreted to serve one narrative over another. The stories I told may have been factually true, but the facts of a life don't carry meaning in themselves. We give them meaning when we string them together in one direction instead of another, emphasizing some moments and omitting others. It took a humiliating conversation with Ricky for me to begin to see how my story functioned to serve a particular agenda.

The summer after my freshman year in college, I was sexually assaulted by my old youth minister. At that time, I thought rape was a thing that happened when a stranger in a ski mask tackled a woman in a dark alley and violently forced himself on her. I didn't know how to make sense of an unwanted sexual encounter with someone I trusted. I told Ricky and my small group leader at Living Hope, but I didn't get professional help. We swept it under the rug. There was no justice, no time to heal. Within six months, however, the rape was incorporated into my testimony. I don't remember who came up with the idea, but most narrative decisions were made together, so I imagine it was something Ricky and I agreed upon. What I still vividly remember is the conversation I had with Ricky one night when I decided not to share that story.

"You did a good job sharing your testimony," Ricky said once we were ten or fifteen minutes into our drive home.

"Oh yeah, thanks. I felt good about it."

After a pause, he continued: "I really regret that you didn't talk about the rape."

I swallowed hard and looked out the window, taking long, slow breaths.

"Well, I didn't want to," I said, feeling nervous and brave. "It's never felt right. I haven't fully processed it. I haven't healed from it. I don't want my whole life to be up for public consumption, and you know, I can choose not to share some of the most vulnerable details of my life with people who don't know me."

"It just takes some of the power out of your story when you don't share it," he said as if he were directing a movie with characters rather than sitting with a twenty-two-year-old still reeling from a traumatic event.

I looked out the window and gave myself permission not to fill the awkward silence. The story was mine. The trauma was mine, and I alone would bear the emotional weight of it when it was shared. It wasn't fodder for a sensational testimony. Besides, it was misleading to incorporate the rape into my ex-gay testimony. I knew I was gay when I was thirteen years old—prior to meeting Turner and long before I was raped. The way we constructed the pieces of my life served an agenda, even if we didn't directly connect the dots. They hinted at the lie that gay adults prey on children, recruiting otherwise straight kids to turn them queer. It reinforced false teachings that people are gay because of sexual abuse. It conveniently supported the idea that lesbians seek comfort in the arms of other women because they were hurt by men. As naive as I still was at that time, my gut said something was off.

A few months before graduation, I became friends with a couple of guys from my school. They were my first real connection to people outside of Living Hope since I had come out to my mom in high school, and it struck me that my life was not normal. My best and only friend was a forty-three-year-old man who was my pastor, therapist, boss, best friend, and father figure all rolled into one. I did not know the last names, or any identifying information, of all the peers I counted among my closest friends. And my entire life revolved around trying not to be gay.

After graduation, my friends convinced me to move to Dallas so we could hang out more often. "Listen, Ju-Ju-Bird," my friend Tyler teased one afternoon. "You can still drive to Arlington for meetings as often as you want. But if you're this anxious about moving twenty miles away from an anonymous support group where you don't even know people's last names, you may want to ask yourself if you're part of a cult."

Tyler was right. It was time for me to take the leap out of Ricky's nest. I packed all of my belongings into my tan Toyota Camry and moved into a spare room in a young married couple's home in East Dallas. Some nights went exactly as I imagined: we hung out on front porches, drank cheap Texas beer, and processed big spiritual questions together. The idea that same-sex relationships might be morally permissible was too scary for me to entertain, but I had other questions.

I was in the early stages of adjusting to the idea of evolution, as opposed to a literal reading of Genesis that said God created the earth in seven days roughly six thousand years ago. I still believed God manipulated the hands of biblical writers to ensure the words were written verbatim onto the pages, straight from the mind of God. But it was just beginning to occur to me that, since the Bible contradicts itself, we who interpret it do the imaginative work of making it cohere according to our specific ideas. That's why we have more than ninety thousand different denominations in the United States alone: we disagree about what these words, written more than two thousand years ago in a vastly different culture, mean for us today in our context. Some moments in conversations over beers, I started to consider the possibility that my faith tradition was based on one reading of Scripture among many other sincere interpretations of the ancient text. Then I would swing back to the familiar belief that we had the absolute truth, and we were soldiers enlisted in the war against those who peddled lies.

To cope with the anxiety my crisis of faith induced, I resurrected an old eating disorder. There was a time in college when I quit eating altogether and dropped down to eighty-nine pounds. That kind of rapid weight loss drew too much attention to my body, though. People noticed and asked questions. I figured out that binging and purging was easier to hide. That's when I started sneaking into our kitchen to steal my roommates' food at night. One evening, a housemate baked a pan of homemade energy bars that looked like a sheet cake, with oats, nuts, dried fruit, and chocolate chips. When she woke up the next morning, only a quarter of the pan was left. Another night, I sat cross-legged with my back to the refrigerator, opened a fresh half gallon of chocolate chip cookie dough ice cream, and finished it in the same sitting. It was cathartic to vomit the ice cream in the hours that followed, purging my body of the sugar, carbs, and calories, tears streaming down my face as I propped my elbows on the toilet and buried my head in my hands. After I finished throwing up, I went for a five-mile run through downtown Dallas in the dark.

I didn't know how to process my crisis, the sense of loss and confusion. Outside of Living Hope, away from Ricky and my mom, I didn't know who I was. I didn't know who I was allowed to be, and I was afraid of who I was becoming. I was anxious about where my questions would take me. Fundamentalism was a coherent system that dictated my life to me: it told me who I was and how I was to live, every moment of every day. It gave me a rulebook that laid out a path for me to be objectively good. When one part of the system was called into question, it brought up a series of related questions that threatened to bring the whole house down. The foundation upon which my life and identity were built began to shake, and I couldn't cope with the thought that the whole house—everything I believed to be true and all the relationships that held me together—might come crashing down.

A few months after my move to Dallas, I called Ricky, crying. He offered a solution: Living Hope had just purchased a duplex that would become the Hope House, a live-in program for guys who struggled with same-sex attractions. He could open one side of it up to guys in the ministry, and then Living Hope's women's director and I could live on the other side. The house was just down the street from Ricky's; he passed it every morning on his drive to the church. I could be close to him again. I could join him for speaking gigs and go grocery shopping with him on weekends, just like old times.

6

My choice to move into the Hope House was a choice to double down on the ex-gay way. *Maybe the doubts I experienced were spiritual attacks*, I thought. *Maybe the questions that haunted me were signs of my rebellious nature.* What if the anxiety I felt was the result of me running away from my calling, like the prophet Jonah who was swallowed up by a whale when he ignored God's command to go to Nineveh? Maybe what I needed was to recommit myself to Living Hope—to take on more responsibility as a leader.

On one side of the duplex, Amber and I lived fairly normal lives. I edited Living Hope's monthly newsletter in exchange for free rent, but I didn't have any leadership responsibilities beyond that. I started working toward a master's in English and waited tables at a pub in the Bishop Arts District west of downtown Dallas to pay for school. When you tell people you're studying English in grad school, everyone asks if you want to teach, which is another way of saying the degree is useless outside of academia. I didn't intend to *use* the degree, though. I wanted to learn. After a childhood education of fundamentalist homeschooling followed by indoctrination at a Baptist college, I was ready to wrestle with big questions, and I've always processed questions best through stories.

On the other side of the Hope House lived three guys in their early to midtwenties. Their arrangement was more structured: they had curfews, they met with Ricky weekly, and they were required to send him their journal entries every evening. Most of them moved in because they had been "in the lifestyle," Living Hope's shorthand for dating or having sex with other men. On Sundays, the Hope House guys and I all had lunch at Ricky's house, where we usually lingered long after the meal was over. In the two years I spent in the Hope House, somewhere around eight or nine different guys cycled through. And while I functioned as a sort of sister to most of them, there was one in particular who truly captured my heart.

Brandon was a tall, broad-shouldered, baby-faced nineteen-year-old from a rural Texas town. He first met Ricky when he was in high school. When his parents found out he was sexually involved with men, they scheduled an appointment with Ricky and made the long drive to meet with him as a family. Brandon kept sleeping with guys, though. He didn't want to be gay: he was a masculine guy from a small town, where the church was the center of the community and guns were a status symbol. Guys in those communities weren't supposed to be soft. After suppressing his desires for months at a time, he would suddenly slip out of the house unannounced to binge on anonymous sex with men he met online.

I adored Brandon from the moment I met him. Brandon, with his thick southern accent, who drove a pickup truck and wore baseball caps backward, had an enormous heart. When a kitten showed up in our backyard, Brandon set out a bowl of milk and made a kitten-sized bed out of blankets and soft towels. On a walk one day, he discovered that a homeless man named James lived in the woods about a half mile from our house, so Brandon stopped by James's tent with gas station snacks with regularity. Because Brandon was insecure in his skin and quiet in groups, most people found him intimidating and hard to read. I adored the sensitive soul beneath his tough facade.

Brandon and I shared a wall on separate sides of the duplex. On nice nights, we sometimes knocked softly on the wall to see if the other was up for a rooftop chat. Then we climbed out of our windows and sat side by side, smoking cigarettes and stargazing as we processed our big questions. Brandon was starting to read books that said Christians should prioritize the poor and the oppressed. The authors wrote about a Christianity that wasn't about following a list of rules—it was about generosity and justice. He was moved by the idea of a religion that was less political, a faith that was based on grace. But he couldn't get past the dogma, especially the teaching that said people like him were an abomination. He couldn't get over the sense of shame he felt in his muscular, queer body.

Then one night, Brandon slipped out of his window and didn't knock on mine. He walked a mile down Division Street, where motels and windowless bars lit up the sky with neon lights, and he strolled into the one that had a tiny rainbow flag outside. He went home with two older men that night and stayed with them for a few weeks. About a month later, Ricky told us Brandon called his parents to tell them that he was safe and he had a job at a strip club in the queer neighborhood in Dallas. It would be a long time before I'd see him again.

o o o

As I grappled with the sorrows and occasional joys of life in the Hope House, my relationship with my mom continued spiraling, so I leaned into my relationship with my dad. In his second career as a high school history teacher, he asked thought-provoking questions about the things I was learning. He was never surprised by my questions. When I voiced confusion over how to interpret Genesis, wondering if it should be read more as poetry than history, he seemed to agree. When I anxiously asked about the numerous ways the Bible contradicts itself, my dad didn't seem worried. His faith had a lot of room for mystery.

At some point when I was in college, my mom found out that my dad and I occasionally met up for meals and talked on the phone. My dad brought it up casually: "Now, onto something logistical," he said as we wrapped up one of our lunches. "Your mom goes through your phone bill, line by line, every month, and she was not happy to see my number on there a few times. She wants to know everything we talk about and why I didn't tell her. She worries we talk about her. I'm just putting that on your radar so you can be aware of it and think about maybe getting a separate phone. Until then, how about I call you from my school phone when we're going to talk so it won't show up on your bill?"

On my drive back to the Hope House that day, I wondered how deep my mom's insecurity must have run for her to feel the need to monitor my relationship with my dad. What kind of anguish she must have felt to believe she had to compete for her kids' love, to split us up into teams—Mom's side against Dad's. My mom's irrational fear that the rest of the family talked about her became a self-fulfilling prophecy. Her behavior warranted discussion and intervention: her increasingly dangerous coping mechanisms, her refusal to respect our individual boundaries, her efforts to either cut off or control the conversations between family members that didn't include her.

I wasn't sure about the way my dad was going about it, though. Why did we need to tiptoe around her, getting new phones or calling each other from different lines? Why didn't we tell her that, yes, we were in conversation because fathers and daughters sometimes talk to each other without a mother's supervision? I assumed it was because she would respond with an emotional outburst. She would likely wail, maybe throw a lamp or break a plate. It would be uncomfortable but honest. I wondered how sustainable this false sense of peace was, predicated on white lies. How far would we bend over backward before we would snap?

Over the next few years, as his relationship with my mom deteriorated and her erratic behavior spiraled further, my dad grew more desperate. He insisted we actively lie to her about our interactions. On one of my birthdays in my early twenties, he took me out to lunch to celebrate. Like most of our hangouts in those years, our time together ended with him wrapping me up in a hug and saying, "I love you" and, without fail, "Now remember, this lunch didn't happen." I had come to accept the terms of our arrangement, but it was jarring to receive a call from my parents' house later that evening: "Happy birthday!" they said in unison. Then my dad asked what I did to celebrate that day, as if we hadn't seen each other a few hours earlier, as if it was the most natural thing in the world for me to cover his lie with another one of my own.

o o o

Exodus International reached out to me during my time living in the Hope House. They wanted me to move up to the ex-gay big league. They asked me to give my testimony on the main stage during one of the general sessions at their national conference. Shortly after the Exodus conference, their leaders reached out again, asking if I would join them for an upcoming Love Won Out conference. These were one-day conferences they did six to eight times a year in churches across the country. If I was up for it, they would pay to fly me out, give me an honorarium of $250, and add me to a lineup that included Alan Chambers, the president of Exodus, and household ex-gay names like Joe Dallas and Anne Paulk.

I took the stage at those conferences wearing frumpy plaid shirts tucked into wide-leg jeans that almost entirely covered my Toms shoes. Conference days were the only times I wore my hair down. For some reason, I equated wearing my hair down with femininity, so when I put gel in my hair and scrunched it into a curly frizz, I wondered if the audience would be able to see Christ shining through me. The makeup was evidence that I wasn't hard-hearted anymore, I thought. Jesus had softened me. He was changing me.

It was 2011 when I started sharing my testimony along-side Exodus's speaking team, and by that point, many old-timers (including Ricky) believed Alan Chambers was taking Exodus in a controversial direction. In public speeches, Alan started saying things like "The opposite of homosexuality is not heterosexuality—it's holiness." In those circles, it was a bold claim, a sharp turn from Exodus's former claims that one could experience "freedom from homosexuality" and become straight.

Alan also set off a firestorm at a conference of fully affirm-ing LGBTQ Christians that year when he went on record as saying, "The majority of people that I have met, and I would say the majority meaning 99.9 percent of them, have not experienced a change in their orientation." He conceded that gay people do not become straight through conversion therapy. They might choose to identify in a different way, labeling themselves "same-sex attracted" instead of gay, and they might choose not to have sexual relationships with people of the same sex, but their orientation doesn't change. They're still gay, according to the dictionary's definition. Alan's statements implied one could live a holy life (through singleness and celibacy) even if their orientation didn't change, whereas many in the ex-gay universe believed holiness necessarily entailed a shift in attractions. Under those circumstances and in that light, I didn't feel dishonest when I shared my testimony. I was allowed to say I was dictionary-definition gay.

Around the time I started speaking with Exodus, I accepted a full-time job working with high school students at a mentoring program in West Dallas. On a whim, I had volunteered to be a counselor at their annual summer camp to spend quality time with a student I was mentoring, and by the end of that week, the kids won my heart. By Christmas, I was on staff. My new job gave me the push I needed to move out of the Hope House for good. I also still had a few courses left in grad school, which took up most of my evenings. For the first time in almost a decade, I couldn't make it to Living Hope's support group meetings on Thursday nights. I occasionally went to Ricky's for lunch on Sundays, but eventually, even that became too big of a time commitment between work and school. Or maybe they served as convenient excuses to pull away? In the same way you need new friends, hobbies, and distractions when you go through a big breakup, I knew

I had to fill the void left by Living Hope. Once I had a circle of friends and a life outside of the ex-gay universe, I was able to answer big questions about identity and community that I previously found exclusively at Living Hope.

With the move to Dallas came a change of churches. I was surprised—even a little alarmed—to find a home in a large Episcopal church called Church of the Incarnation. They held traditional services in a towering cathedral and an evening service in a quaint chapel that seated about two hundred people. It was a more contemporary service, which was an easier transition for me coming from Evangelical churches. The sermons were shorter in the Episcopal Church. Where Evangelical services centered on the pastor and his long sermons, the Episcopal Church was rooted in the text of a shared liturgy and the Eucharist.

Incarnation was the first church I attended where I felt like my faith could breathe. On the Sundays when I wasn't sure if Christianity was true at all, I could slip into the back row and let the prayers of the people wash over me, carrying me down a stream that started with the apostles and saints more than two thousand years ago.

The community of Episcopal churches in Dallas is more conservative than most in the country, which added to its allure for me at that time. I was too scared to go to churches that flew rainbow flags—I feared they had strayed from the truth. Incarnation didn't discuss same-sex relationships, but I learned over time that their priests were divided on the issue: some believed God blessed same-sex relationships and that the church should too, and some held more conservative views. While they didn't marry same-sex couples, they did warmly embrace the queer people in their congregation, even welcoming us into leadership in various capacities. It was the refuge I needed in that tumultuous season.

Life in Dallas felt larger. My friends outside of Living Hope would accept me regardless of whether I was gay or straight, Christian or agnostic, on a fitness kick or in a drinking binge. Our conversations didn't revolve around my "struggle" with same-sex attractions. We talked about the latest books we had read or the big questions we turned over in our minds throughout our days. Between my new church and my more open-minded friends, I started to think there might be a place for me to belong outside the boundaries of the fundamentalist universe.

That year in Dallas was also the time I began to face the devastating consequences that ex-gay teaching had on my friends from earlier years.

It started when I ran into Kevin on the streets of Dallas. Athletic and handsome, Kevin was a competitive gymnast turned triathlete when he arrived at Living Hope. Like most of us, he set out to be a good Christian boy: he attended my Baptist college, and he was always eager to give a testimony about God's faithfulness in his life. At some point Kevin disappeared, and eventually Ricky informed us that he had gone into the "lifestyle." Ricky said Kevin had given in to his flesh and that we needed to pray he would hit rock bottom sooner rather than later and come back home.

I first spotted Kevin with a cup in his hand at a busy intersection downtown. I rolled down my window and yelled, "Kevin?!" He was hardly recognizable: His hair had thinned significantly, as if he were a twenty-six-year-old with a sixty-five-year-old's hairline. His face was dotted with open sores, his clothes baggy and torn. It was a stark contrast to the clean-cut Kevin I knew in college. His face lit up when he saw me, but the light turned green before we got a chance to talk, so I waved at him from my car window and told him I missed him as I drove off.

A couple of months later, I ran into him again outside of my neighborhood grocery store. My gaze immediately went to his teeth: the ones that weren't missing had jagged edges. "Brother!" I said after a long embrace. "You doing alright?"

"Honestly, no," he said. "Do you have time to talk?"

Over the next hour, he hurried through the horror story he had been living in the years since I'd last seen him. He said he got into some unhealthy cycles during his time at Living Hope. He would suppress his sexuality for as long as possible, relying on prayer, Scripture, and accountability to keep him from expressing his sexuality, and then he would binge. He'd go to bathhouses and hook up with strangers—the riskier, the more satisfying. Then he'd return to Living Hope, remorseful, and confess what he'd done, only to repeat the cycle again a few months later. He felt deeply ashamed, like there was something uniquely broken about him that kept him from healing.

"One night on a binge, a guy pulled out a pipe and asked if I'd ever smoked ice," he told me that afternoon. "I said I had and asked him to pass it. I figured, what the fuck? I already felt like shit about myself, so why not try it this once?"

Kevin was hooked. From the first night he smoked it, he said all he could think about was the next time he could get meth. Insecurities had plagued him his entire life: he was insecure about his body, his sexuality, his personality, his place in

God's family. Meth made him feel confident and cool. Even though he had to couch surf and sleep on the streets, meth made him feel alive.

Before we parted ways, he asked if I had any extra cash. "I swear to God I'll pay you back next time I see you," he promised.

I'm not sure how we parted—I only remember him sliding the salt and pepper shakers off the table and into his bag before he got up to head for the door.

Ex-gay leaders had a narrative that explained stories like Kevin's: that's what happens when you choose to give in to your flesh, they would say. The gay lifestyle is full of drugs and binge sex with strangers. They never said people like Kevin were driven to destructive behaviors because of shame-based cycles of repression and religious prohibition. No, people like Kevin who embraced the lifestyle embodied the ethics and ideals of the LGBTQ community.

Ex-gay leaders denied the existence of a loving, committed same-sex relationship. According to leaders in my community, true love was only possible among heterosexual Christians. If someone claimed to romantically love someone of the same sex, they were told they were mistaken. It was emotional dependency or enmeshment they confused for love. Over time, the ex-gay leaders said, people in same-sex relationships would grow to consume and abuse each other.

Had Kevin's story been an isolated one, I might have gone on believing the ex-gay narrative about people "in the lifestyle." But a few months later, my phone rang, jolting me out of denial. For reasons I will never know, I answered a call from an unknown number.

"Julie?" a voice said on the other end. "It's Brandon."

"Brandon, like, my *brother* Brandon?!"

"Yeah, are you free? I'm on a pay phone at a gas station and things are really bad."

"What do you need, man? Anything, I'm here."

"I don't know," his voice cracked. He sounded like he was shuddering. "People are chasing me. Everyone is screaming, and I'm really scared."

Through a few more focused questions, I figured out where he was and told him to sit down on the curb by the gas station. I was on my way.

As soon as I pulled up to the Shell station in the heart of Dallas's gayborhood, I saw Brandon slouched on the curb, his arms folded over his knees to make a pillow for his head.

"Brother!" I cried, leaping out of my car. "It's so good to *see* you, man!"

Brandon leapt up and wrapped me in his arms. "I've never been so happy to see someone in my whole life, Julie."

"Man, it's *you*," I said, pulling him close again.

We ducked into my car and I turned toward him, gently placing my hand on his shoulder.

"What's going on, B?"

"It's these guys," he said, burying his forehead in his hand. "They're coming for me and they're relentless!"

He didn't have anything with him—just the plain white T-shirt and jeans that sagged from his skinny frame.

"Brandon, are you on something right now? Do you think you might need to go to the hospital?"

"No, I don't need to go to the hospital," he said, scratching his scalp with both of his hands. "I just need to get away from them!"

"Hey, you're safe now," I said, moving my hand back and forth from his shoulder to his upper back to soothe him. "They're not gonna get us, B."

Eventually, I recruited a few leaders from Living Hope to help care for Brandon. When we got him to the emergency room, the doctor explained he was experiencing severe psychosis related to meth abuse. He needed to detox. It was going to get worse before it got better. First, he would spiral further into hallucinations, but in a few days, the healing process would begin. The doctor offered information on recovery programs and told us Brandon was lucky to be alive.

Over the years, both Brandon and Kevin put in the hard work to get clean. Kevin recently got a new set of teeth, and he started training for triathlons again. He told me some mornings he wakes up and feels his throat tingle the way it used to after he had just inhaled, and the yearning for meth never leaves. But he says he's proud of the man he's become. Brandon found strength in a faith community that embraced him. They've taken different paths to recovery, but it's been a long road for both of them.

Dozens of other acquaintances and friends were ravaged by ex-gay teaching. I could not yet see myself in their stories—I still thought my cycles of self-harm were signs that I was deficient in some way—but it was gutting to see how my friends suffered. There was Tim, who brought his pills to a group meeting at Living Hope and then attempted suicide shortly after. There was Jamie, with a buzz cut, who told me she'd been cutting and that sometimes when she cut the soft underside of her forearm, she felt the impulse to press the knife deeper until she hit a vein to end it all. There was Kyle, who was so consumed with self-hatred that one night he took a knife to his chest and carved the letters *F-A-G*.

I understand most people hear these stories and just see names. They see statistics. But Brandon, Kevin, and Kyle are not simply names or statistics. They are human beings who were nursed as babies, who grew up with dreams to make the world a more beautiful place. They have rich inner lives and vivid imaginations. When religious leaders came along and made them loathe their bodies, made them feel like a source of disgust to their families, they robbed each and every one of these humans of their one precious life. No matter how much Kyle has healed from the trauma, he still sees *FAG* on his chest every time he steps out of the shower. He will never get a new body. Whatever healing he's experienced is not a redemption story. It is not romantic. It's a gritty, heart-wrenching story of survival.

As I encountered the consequences of ex-gay teaching, I was horrified to consider the role I had played in perpetuating a message that led to death: relational death, emotional death, spiritual death, and in some cases, physical death.

We were wrong, I thought to myself. I knew it in my gut, but I didn't know how to process it. In a community that denied personal experience as a source of wisdom, we were always told, "Don't let your experience influence your theology; don't trust your feelings." I didn't know how to tease out the dogmatic teachings from the truth, but I was very clear on one thing: I refused to believe God was "glorified" by the ruin of queer kids' lives.

Exactly one year after I joined Exodus's speaking team, I worked up the courage to email Alan Chambers and the team at Exodus. I said I was done. I was anxious, overwhelmed, and sorry that I wouldn't be able to fulfill my contract. I told them my orientation hadn't changed, and I was starting to think we were responsible for so much of the damage done to queer kids in the name of God. I couldn't do it anymore.

It took me hours to send it. I sat on my bed, staring at the email, crying, praying, hoping my instincts were right. Then with a wave of courage, I hit "send." Immediately, I felt free.

For what felt like the first time in my life, I followed my conscience instead of the religious authorities, and I knew the decision was right. I didn't know what it meant for my theology or how it would affect my relationship with my Christian community. Honestly, I was still scared of hell. But I finally claimed the space to figure it out.

A couple of hours later, Alan responded. He asked me if I could join them one last time for the upcoming conference in Atlanta. He wanted to have dinner to discuss my concerns.

Perhaps it was my people-pleasing tendencies or maybe the result of being formed in a fundamentalist system where leaders had boundless moral authority, but I felt incapable of saying no to him. Ever the guilt-ridden human, I said I'd see him in Atlanta the next month.

7

"I can't do it anymore," I said to Alan Chambers as I pushed pasta around my plate with a fork. At twenty-six years old, I had traveled to regional conferences with the Exodus team for a full year to share my testimony. Much like the arrangement with Living Hope, my story was used to illustrate the points ex-gay leaders made in their presentations.

"I mean, I still have traditional views of sex and marriage," I reassured Alan, "but this ex-gay stuff doesn't work. I've been at this for eight years and I'm still, like, really gay. Ex-gay teaching has pummeled people I love. They're hooked on meth and cut off from their families and suicidal. It's not okay! I can't do it anymore."

I exhaled. Then I searched his face for a reaction.

His response was completely unexpected: "Honestly, Julie, I'm sick of this too. I've sat across from countless people with your story, and I'm starting to come to terms with the damage we've done. I don't think Exodus can be reformed—I think it needs to end."

I was stunned. I was prepared for a wide range of possible responses from him, but not that.

He went on to tell me he was exhausted by the culture wars. What was it to him if two people of the same sex loved each other and wanted to be together? The Holy Spirit could speak to them if God had different plans for them—it wasn't his job to police other people's sex lives. It's time for Christians to be known by what we're for, he said, not what we're against. He wanted out of the business of judgment and condemnation—he was ready to preach a message of grace.

Then came his request: "Would you consider speaking at our conferences a little while longer and just telling the truth? Tell people exactly what you just told me. We need someone to tell the truth."

I looked down at the table and tried to make sense of what I heard.

"You mean you want me to tell people who come to ex-gay conferences that I'm still gay and that ex-gay teaching is harmful?"

"Yeah, basically," he said. "I think you can be a powerful influence for people who haven't heard the painful stories you and I have heard. It'll just be one more year. Then you can move on with your life and be done with this mess."

Cleaning up Exodus's mess was the last thing I wanted to do with the next year of my life, but I felt guilty for the part I had played in perpetuating ex-gay narratives. Plus, I knew I was uniquely positioned to be a force for change: by that point, I had spent nine years in Exodus ministries. I had seen, first-hand, how they harmed people. As a blogger and speaker, I knew that my platform positioned me to reach those who most needed to hear it. Slouched in the booth across from Alan, I felt incapable of saying no to his request.

A couple of months later, I wrote a blog post for Exodus's website that outlined the problems with telling gay people they need to become straight. I said I hadn't changed and that most of my friends were still gay. I apologized for the way Exodus wreaked havoc on countless people's lives. I spoke directly to the LGBTQ people who had been harmed by Exodus, telling them they deserved better than the shame-based messages of "leave homosexuality or leave the church." Here's an excerpt from that post:

> To those of you who have been disillusioned, damaged, or downright shamed for being gay: know it breaks the heart of God and there are many of us at Exodus grieving on your behalf. I also want you to know I earnestly pray for you. I don't know many of your names or faces, but I pray the Lord will meet you and bring healing from the pain that was caused. I pray that one day we can hear your stories—stories of encountering the scandalous love of Christ in the most unexpected places. And I want you to know now what I wish you had known when you passed through before: Jesus loves you right now, right where you are.

The post exploded.

Conservatives wanted to know why someone was speaking on behalf of the largest ex-gay organization in the world saying most of the people who came through Exodus hadn't changed. And what was up with the apology? What did it mean? Was this just a rogue young leader saying she personally feels sorry, or did she represent the leadership of Exodus International?

Queer people were pleasantly surprised. Activists still called for Exodus to shut down and fully affirm same-sex love, but they were glad to hear someone acknowledge the fact that gays didn't change and that conversion therapy was harmful.

The day the post went live, a man named Michael Bussee reached out. He told me he facilitated a group for ex-gay survivors on Facebook. Michael was one of the original founders of Exodus in 1976 who left a few years after starting it when he fell in love with a cofounder. He devoted the rest of his life to creating safe places for ex-gay survivors to find community and support. In his message to me, he said he was shocked to hear someone from Exodus apologize to those they had harmed. He said some of the people in his group would like to take me up on my offer to hear their stories.

I joined the group and was immediately overwhelmed by the depth of the pain people brought into the conversation. With more than seventy-five members, I couldn't keep up with all of the stories of family rejection, suicide attempts, homelessness, and drug addiction. Exodus had ruined their lives. They would never get back the years they lost to coping with the pain of being told they were demon-possessed or a disgrace to their loved ones.

I quickly reached out to Randy Thomas, the vice president of Exodus, and Alan to tell them they needed to be in the group. I was only one person, and I wasn't on Exodus's staff. I didn't have the authority to speak for Exodus the way they did. And honestly, I didn't have the emotional capacity to hold all of the survivors' pain and rage by myself. This was their job.

Three weeks later, I found myself in the basement of a church building in Los Angeles, where I sat in a circle with a dozen ex-gay survivors as a television crew hovered around us. A journalist named Lisa Ling had been intrigued by the changes she saw at Exodus in the years leading up to this show. She had interviewed Alan several times over the years, and while she held him accountable for the harm Exodus caused, she was also sympathetic toward him as a human being. In her interviews, she sought to see the world through the lens of a conservative Christian whose sexual orientation was at odds with their religious beliefs, and she told the stories with compassion.

The filming lasted several hours. For the first couple of hours, ex-gay survivors shared their stories. They talked about growing up in conservative communities and wanting so badly to be good. They read journal entries from their teenage years, when they begged God to cure them and wondered why they hadn't received the healing they were promised. Many in the room had married people of the opposite sex, and they described the guilt they carried about the pain they inflicted upon their children and former spouses. They couldn't love their families the way they deserved to be loved when they were hiding and lying and suppressing their true selves. One theme that ran through every story was a deep sense of betrayal by the people they had trusted growing up.

That was the first time I remember identifying more with ex-gay survivors than Exodus leaders. I had previously been moved by the stories of friends who were hurt by Exodus, but I hadn't seen myself in their stories. As I sat in the circle on that Saturday morning in Los Angeles, I listened to these people tell my own story: the story of being an earnest kid who wanted to be good—a story of fear, exploitation, and betrayal. I wasn't as angry as they were, but I wondered if maybe it was because I wasn't as honest with myself as they were.

This sudden realization that I was also a survivor and that my suffering mattered, too, came in part as the result of a year of therapy. Shortly after I moved to Dallas, I started seeing a therapist because I had a hunch that I might have a little emotional baggage to work through. "I wouldn't say I have an eating disorder," I told my therapist when we first met. "I make sure to eat a solid four hundred calories a day." I told her I often canceled plans to work out instead and that I was having emotional withdrawals from living just thirty minutes away from Ricky.

Sydney was a Christian, but she was a licensed professional therapist, and she knew conversion therapy was bogus and harmful. She didn't have an agenda for where I landed on moral questions related to same-sex relationships. Her goal, as my therapist, was to help me live an integrated life: one where my convictions and actions were in alignment, and I had a strong sense of self.

"Listen, Julie, I don't know what the way forward will look like for you, but I know you're going to figure it out in relationship, not isolation."

Sydney helped me begin the process of disentangling myself from both my mom and Ricky. She showed me the value of setting boundaries—especially with authority figures who I'd given unfettered access to the deepest parts of myself. She helped me work through the immense guilt I felt for setting boundaries with my mom and convinced me my value was not tied to other peoples' approval of me. She made me feel like I mattered.

So when I found myself in that church basement in Los Angeles, sitting in a circle with a dozen ex-gay survivors, I suddenly understood I had also been abused by this system. My self-destructive tendencies weren't a sign of inherent brokenness—they were a direct response to trauma.

Other survivors were worth fighting for in my effort to end Exodus, and I was worth fighting for too. I would continue speaking at Exodus conferences, but something had fundamentally shifted—I now aligned my story with those who stood firmly against everything Exodus International represented.

I got in my rental car when I left the circle of ex-gay survivors and drove thirty minutes in the wrong direction, too disoriented and emotionally unstable to find my way back to my hotel. The next morning, after a short interview with Lisa Ling, I went to the airport, boarded a plane, and wept the entire flight back to Texas.

My mom was disappointed about my role in the narrative change happening at Exodus. "You don't believe God is powerful enough to heal you?" she asked me on the phone one evening, soon after she heard about the changes at Exodus. I tried to explain that, sure, if God created the whole world, then God could change my sexual orientation. God didn't seem to change many people's sexual orientations, though. In fact, God didn't intervene in a lot of things: world hunger, stage-four cancer, war.

Obviously, being queer is in no way comparable to cancer or war, but I knew my mom saw each of them as problems that warranted intervention from God.

I was no longer interested in theoretical questions about what God *could* do. I was interested in what happened to actual human beings in the real world. The more important question, to me, became, Does this teaching lead to harm or healing? I didn't think Jesus would advocate for anything that harmed people, especially people who were pushed to the margins of the church and society. Ex-gay teaching clearly caused harm.

At twenty-seven years old, I was a couple of years away from Living Hope and a year into therapy. I rarely went to group meetings anymore. Ricky and I met for coffee once every few months, where we mainly caught each other up on our lives. Our relationship settled into the rhythms of a typical parent/child relationship when the child becomes an adult: I knew I could always count on Ricky to be there for me in moments of need, but the enmeshment of my late teens and early twenties had evolved into something else. When we met up with each other, we shared *about* our lives rather than sharing our lives *with* one another.

Like my mom, Ricky was concerned about my involvement in the changes happening at Exodus: "If the gospel can save us from sin and transform every part of our lives, then why wouldn't that include our sexuality?" Ricky challenged me. "Don't you think it's wrong to say, 'Here, God, you can take over every part of my life *except* for my sexuality . . . I don't believe you have the power to change that.'"

"Ricky, haven't you listened to all of the stories of people who didn't change, who say this teaching harmed them? Do you think they're just making shit up to stir up trouble?"

Ricky cited recovery rates among alcoholics, saying the majority of people who sought treatment for their addiction returned to their unhealthy coping mechanisms. "Wide is the road that leads to destruction," he would say to me, quoting Scripture. "But narrow is the road that leads to life, and few find it. It's right there in the Bible. We shouldn't be surprised that the majority of people fall back into their old patterns."

"Okay, but don't you think being gay is different than having an addiction?" I asked. "Can you at least acknowledge the difference between an orientation and a behavior? A sexual orientation is unchosen. It's morally neutral. We have choices about sex and dating, but we don't choose our attractions or who we love."

"I think it's great that you're not sleeping with women," he said in response. "I do worry about you going around saying you're gay. The stories we tell ourselves are really powerful, and if you're telling yourself you're gay, it'll be a self-fulfilling prophecy."

"Well, I said I was straight for eight years, and that didn't turn out to be a self-fulfilling prophecy, did it?"

We went back and forth like that often in my final years in the ex-gay universe. Things between us were tense. Ricky often said he hoped I would be his legacy and that I would carry the baton on the next leg of the race after he finished. He said he didn't know if I was simply going through a rebellious phase, playing the devil's advocate like a typical twentysomething who's read a few books, or if I was slipping away like so many Living Hope alumni we had known and loved.

In the summer of 2013, two months after the survivor's circle in the LA church basement, I flew to California again for the final Exodus conference. On the opening night of the conference, Alan announced that Exodus was going to shut down. He apologized for his lack of honesty about his ongoing same-sex attractions. He apologized for being an enemy to so many in the LGBTQ community. He mourned the harm ex-gay teaching had caused. He said he wanted to be a peacemaker and that, by the end of the month, Exodus would cease to be a living, breathing organism.

For the rest of the conference, the Exodus team was in crisis mode. Attendees were in need of spiritual care, and the Exodus team couldn't keep up with the media requests. Alan asked if I could go on Wolf Blitzer and meet with a reporter from the *New York Times*. Friends from home bombarded me with texts, wondering whether I still stood for truth. Ricky was disappointed. My mom was frantic. I was exhausted.

The final Exodus conference took place exactly ten years after my first one. For the first half of my time in ex-gay ministry, I would say I was a true believer in the process. The second half was a long quest to escape. First, I tried to run away and then dragged myself back like a scared child returning to an abusive home. For the last couple of years, I fought for freedom for myself and my friends by trying to change the organization from within.

I was, at times, manipulated. At other points, complicit. And in the end, I was brave. It's tempting to try to squeeze my years in conversion therapy into one of those categories. It would help me locate myself on the spectrum of good and evil. But life isn't always that tidy. Many of us find ourselves, at various points, a victim, a villain, and a champion.

I'm learning to have compassion for my younger self—not just the sixteen-year-old who knew she had no good options but also the twenty-four-year-old who kept smiling for the cameras, despite her misgivings. This compassion for all the different versions of myself opens me up to have mercy on those I place squarely in the evil category today. Perhaps they're also victims of a system they have not yet seen for what it truly is. It's not too late for any of us to change.

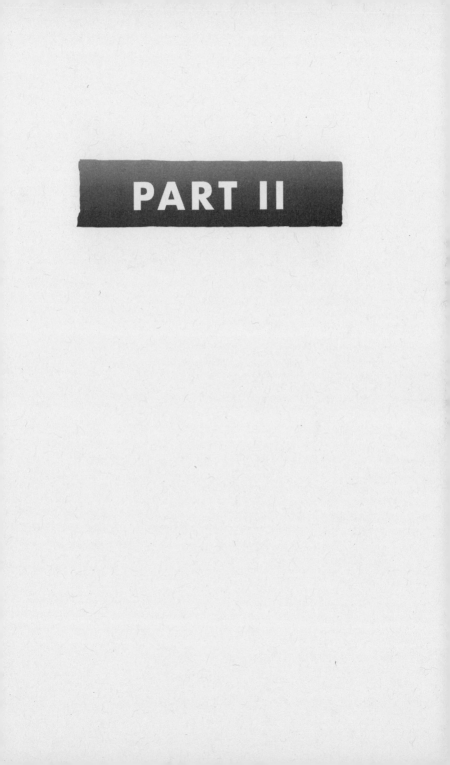

PART II

8

A year after Exodus ended, I got an email from a guy named Gabe Lyons. Gabe was the president of an organization called Q, which sought to curate cutting-edge conversations with renowned pastors, artists, public servants, and activists working at the intersection of faith and the common good. He said he listened to a few of my talks online and read some of my articles about being a celibate lesbian with traditional views of sex and marriage. He was convinced God wanted us to connect. He knew it was last minute, but could I make it to San Francisco in two weeks for an off-the-record roundtable discussion with pastors, business leaders, and key stakeholders in the conversation about LGBTQ rights and religious liberty? They would cover all the costs. He said my voice was vital in these conversations, and they would treat me to the city's finest food and drinks.

Two weeks later, I walked into a private room at a high-end sushi bar and looked through the place cards until I found my name. The table looked like it was set for about eighteen people, and everyone in the room wore finer clothes than I did. As I scanned the room, I understood these were people with power. They were pastors of megachurches and presidents of Christian colleges. One guy said he helped start Twitter. There were PR strategists who represented some of the largest companies in the country, many of them led by conservative Christian executives.

Then there was me. The youngest person in the room by at least a decade, I was one of only two women and the only gay person at the gathering. My discomfort was about more than my sexuality, though. These men had impressive titles, best-selling books, successful companies, and influence in society. They knew how to pronounce all the items on the menu. I had never made more than $40,000 in a year, and all my jobs had allowed me to wear jeans and a T-shirt. I didn't know the language—the unwritten rules—of people with power.

A savvier person would have had questions. Why had they invited me into this elite club? Why was I the only queer person invited into a strategy session with an agenda that worked directly against the broader LGBTQ community? What did they want from me?

I was too innocent (or maybe self-involved) to be suspicious or cynical, though. I felt important. These influencers saw something in me that they wanted. Once again, I was chosen. This time it wasn't by a fringe group that was largely mocked and dismissed by the broader culture. These leaders had clout in the real world among people I admired.

The next morning, I dressed myself in what would become my signature outfit in this new world of important people: a button-up oxford shirt from the Ralph Lauren outlet store; a navy-blue cardigan from the J. Crew outlet store; brown oxford shoes, also from the outlet mall; and my first pair of skinny jeans. Some friends had recently staged an intervention: they informed me that I absolutely could not wear my hair in a frizzy, loose ponytail any longer—I looked like the pitcher of a middle school softball team. And the wide-leg jeans had to go. I needed skinny jeans. If I didn't feel qualified, I was going to at least look qualified, and if I didn't have the money for it, then I would scour outlet malls and secondhand stores to piece together a look to help me pass as someone who might belong in spaces where important people gathered.

When we convened the next morning, Gabe asked everyone to introduce themselves. Then he opened the conversation with some reflections about LGBTQ rights and religious freedom—what he referred to as "the most divisive issue of our day." He said attitudes toward LGBTQ people were rapidly changing. Polls showed the majority of Americans supported same-sex marriage, and recent court rulings reflected these shifting views. Gabe didn't publicly lament the cultural changes, though. He seemed to understand that conservative Christians had an image problem. They were widely perceived to be self-righteous and judgmental because many Evangelical leaders had, in fact, been self-righteous and judgmental.

Pat Robertson, founder of the Christian Coalition, was mainstream enough to give speeches at the Republican National Conventions, and he reflected the views of many conservative Christians. In a fundraising letter in the 1990s, he wrote, "The feminist agenda is not about equal rights for women. It is about a socialist, anti-family political movement that encourages women to leave their husbands, kill their children, practice witchcraft, destroy capitalism and become lesbians."

Jerry Falwell said, "AIDS is not just God's punishment for homosexuals; it is God's punishment for the society that tolerates homosexuals." He added, "The homosexuals are on the march in this country. Please remember, homosexuals do not reproduce! They recruit! And, many of them are after my children and your children."

In response, Gabe gave evangelicalism a makeover. Despite the fact that Gabe himself graduated from Falwell's Liberty University, he seemed to want to make the embarrassing folks look like they were on the fringes of evangelicalism, not real representatives. Sharing his vision for the future, he used words like "winsome" and "flourishing" in presenting the new face of the movement.

"This isn't just about protecting ourselves," Gabe said. "If we're going to convince people we're not homophobic, then we need to stand up for the rights of Muslim neighbors and people of other faiths as well. This is about preserving a pluralistic society where we can all flourish, despite our differences."

Several people who worked in Christian higher education were present, and they said they were catching heat from people in the LGBTQ community because of their policies around marriage and sexuality. Queer students were finding their voices. They organized protests and demonstrations to demand equality for sexual and gender minorities. Administrators at Christian colleges spoke about their fears that LGBTQ students' claims of discrimination might eventually lead to them losing federal funding.

The people at the roundtable gathering clearly sought to be compassionate. One guy in his late twenties said his mom was a lesbian, but he loved her unconditionally, and he had a great relationship with her and her partner. At one point, a best-selling author and megachurch pastor wrinkled his forehead and squinted his eyes as he reflected on how painful it must be to be a same-sex-attracted Christian in the church. We need to do better, he said. These men and women, made in the image of God, deserve *better*.

After lunch, I cautiously waded into the discussion. "If you want to convince people you're not just out to protect yourselves and that you're ready to move beyond the culture wars, maybe you could try advocating for the rights of LGBTQ people to be protected from basic discrimination."

Every last one of them looked me in the eye.

"The church has fought against the gay community at every point in our history," I went on. "Christians stood by during the AIDS crisis. They kicked queer kids out of their homes and churches. Now they fight against protections for LGBTQ people in employment, housing, and health care. Does it really hurt the cause of Christianity if gay people are protected from discrimination when it comes to housing and public accommodations? Seriously, if you fight against LGBTQ rights across the board, it's hard to believe you care about us. You would be wise to find ways to stand with the queer community, for the sake of your own credibility and the integrity of your message, if nothing else."

"Thanks for sharing that, Julie—you make some great points," Gabe said as he scribbled a few notes on the large white paper at the front of the room. Then he posed a new question for the group, steering the conversation in a different direction.

After the meeting ended, one of the guys in the group asked if I wanted to grab a beer before we flew out. Ben was a little older than me (late thirties or early forties), and he was tired. He had also grown up in a conservative Christian community and built a significant platform as a writer and speaker. By the time we were ordering our second beers, we vented more freely about the dynamics in the room that day.

Why was *this* their big issue? Why did Christians pump so much time and energy into managing the gays?

I found myself saying something I never said in professional settings: "When God scans the whole world and sees people dying of hunger and millions displaced by violent wars over money and power, I can't imagine God is wringing his hands over two people of the same sex who love each other. I honestly don't think he cares."

Ben said he felt the same way. But we both knew what happened to Evangelicals who deviated from the approved stance on this issue. We felt like we could do important work within those communities if we stuck around and kept our controversial questions to ourselves.

When we finished our drinks, Ben left for the airport and I made my way over to Oakland, where I had plans to stay with a friend for a few days so we could attend San Francisco's Pride Parade.

I was not prepared for Pride week in San Francisco. If I were to add up all the gays I had seen in the twenty-seven years I had been alive before that weekend, it wouldn't have come close to the number of queers I saw in the streets of San Francisco that week. They wore rainbow panties and leather straps. Men pranced around with nothing but body paint or socks over their penises. I was there because of a complicated relationship with my friend Myles, who at that time went by Amelia.

Amelia and I connected on Facebook years earlier, when a mutual friend said we should be friends. She was in her final semester at an Evangelical college, and I was still involved at Exodus. I could tell from the handful of messages we exchanged that she was smart and adventurous, someone I would be friends with if we lived near one another. She loved Jesus, but she wasn't persuaded by the answers Evangelicals gave her when it came to same-sex relationships. She saw how their theology harmed her queer friends, and she longed for a theology that set them free from self-hatred. She wasn't convinced that a compassionate expression of theology that said their orientation was inherently sinful would move them into that place of freedom. Shortly after college, she got a job at an organization in Kansas that worked for full equality for LGBTQ people, which moved her into a rainbow-painted house that was only a road trip away from me.

In the fall of 2013, we met in person for the first time. She said she would be in Dallas to visit a friend, but I gathered I was the reason for the visit. Even though I was committed to celibacy and she was casually dating other people, we were both aware of the connection between us, with our phone conversations stretching late into the night.

When she rolled up to my apartment and jumped out of her black Ford Focus, I felt a flutter in my chest. And when I hugged her, holding on for a few seconds longer than I did with other women, endorphins pulsed through my body. I felt an excitement, a sense of security, a confidence that the touch wasn't a cause for concern to her, like I feared it concerned most women. I felt at home and alive in my body.

We spent the whole day together. I took her to my favorite bookstore and showed her the neighborhood where I worked. We had pizza and beers at the pub where I was a manager when we first met. We introduced each other to songs that moved us. By the time we got back to my apartment that night, we were both on the high you get after a first date that went better than you thought possible. She snuggled up next to me on the couch, and we forced a little awkward conversation. Then she made the most reasonable move in the world: she leaned in to kiss me.

I had been in training for this moment my entire life, so jerking my head back was my body's natural response to the advance. For years, I was conditioned to have one response to sexual temptation: shut it down. I told her I thought she was great, but that I was not a hypocrite. I said it was getting late and that she should probably make her way back to her friend's house for the night.

When I met with my therapist that week, I expected her to rebuke me for letting things with Amelia go that far. How had I created the conditions for such a close call? While my therapist supported my move away from Exodus and Living Hope, I sensed she believed same-sex relationships weren't God's best for people like me. Her response surprised me.

"Listen, Julie, I don't know what the future holds for you in terms of your sexuality and theology, but I do know you're not going to figure any of this out in isolation. You're going to figure it out in relationships. That doesn't mean you have to date Amelia or sleep with her—what this looks like is up to you—but you've already tried the path of cutting yourself off from close connections, and it seems like it might be time to risk vulnerability in a relationship."

That began my yearlong process of drawing Amelia close and then pushing her away. We were in something like a committed friendship, or a celibate partnership—a relationship that was intimate and romantic in ways, but never sexual, never physical. There were entire months when even that felt too lesbian for me. I feared I was playing with fire.

Still, she loved me—she loved me so much that she was willing to give up sex for the rest of her life if it meant we could share our lives together. I opened myself up to receive that love from her more than I had ever allowed myself to before, but I didn't know how to love her in return. Of the dozens of letters she sent me, with cute doodles on the envelopes, I responded to one.

Our rendezvous in Oakland the weekend of San Francisco's Pride was part of that year we shared. She still lived in Kansas, and I was in Texas, so it seemed serendipitous when we were both going to be in the Bay Area for work that weekend. We booked an Airbnb for a few nights and played house together, both of us testing this unconventional manner of coupling up. I was distant and cold the whole weekend—in part because of my internalized homophobia. But I was also beginning to learn the kinds of things straight folks get to learn through the high school and college dating scene: what kind of person is a good fit once the pheromones wear off. What it's like to be together when our insecurities emerge and we start to get clingy or withdrawn.

Then we went to Pride, and everything spiraled quickly from there. Amelia marched in the parade with her organization, so I was on my own, way outside of my comfort zone. Most of the streets and intersections were blocked off, and it was hard to navigate. People spilled warm beer on me as I pushed my way through crowds of shirtless, sweaty bodies, and I wondered if I was sinning simply by being there. What if someone who knew me from my work saw me? Would they take my presence as an endorsement of the drunken celebration of sexual liberation?

I settled into a spot in the front of a crowd when the parade started and tried to open myself up to the experience. Some parts of it felt benign: The CrossFit community cruised by with a mobile dance party on wheels. Many churches marched in matching T-shirts with banners that expressed variations of "We welcome everyone" and "We are all God's children." But my brain sorted those groups into the "liberal churches," who I was taught were hijacking God's commandment to love, turning it into a license to sin.

I kept my composure until the kink folks started rolling by. There were large men in black harnesses who cracked whips as they walked. Some had leashes attached to skinny, young guys who crawled on all fours in front of them. It felt violent to me, the older men towering over young guys who looked like they were fresh out of high school. As different manifestations of the BDSM, kink, and fetish scene rolled by, my chest tightened, and my stomach turned. I felt scared and unsafe. I worried the men were taking advantage of vulnerable young people who were only looking for a place to belong.

As the participants marched on, all the messages I heard from church leaders about LGBTQ people flooded in: *Homosexuality is a deviant lifestyle. They recruit young people and use them for sex. They're perverse. They're into drugs and violence, always looking for fresh meat to corrupt.*

It didn't occur to me then that straight people were also into kink and BDSM and that it's a sexual scene all kinds of people are drawn to for a range of reasons. Some even see it as an expression of freedom and empowerment.

The groups promoting kink had triggered me. The parade featured far more churches and organizations working to prevent teen bullying than men with whips. But they tapped into my deepest fears about becoming affirming, then sliding down a slippery slope that ended in an expression of sexual liberation that scared me.

Bible verses came to mind: "Although they know God's righteous decree that those who do such things deserve death, they not only continue to do these very things but also approve of those who practice them."

I was overcome with a fear that I was approving of evil simply by being there. I felt an urgent need to flee, to get as far away from the parade as possible. *Maybe Ricky and my mom were right*, I thought. *Maybe things that seem innocent on the surface like the It Gets Better Campaign were simply gateways to depravity.*

After the parade, I walked by booths where advocacy organizations sold T-shirts as I tried to calm myself down. It was hot. I was hungry. I wanted to go home.

"What a time to be alive!" Amelia shouted when we finally found each other.

"Yeah, that was something," I said with restraint. "I'm ready to get out of here."

We started bickering on the train ride, and when we got off at our stop, I let loose.

"Yeah, I absolutely cannot participate in anything that even remotely endorses what I just witnessed," I said. "I know we make fun of Christians for talking about 'the gay lifestyle' as if it's monolithic, but that's the kind of shit they're talking about, and it's real."

"I reject the notion that there is a 'gay lifestyle'!" Amelia replied, making quotation marks with her fingers. "So you saw some people who have different sexual ethics than you, whoop-de-do. There were thousands of people marching, and you could've focused on any of those groups, but you want to pick the most extreme expression of sexual liberation and extrapolate it out to make judgments about the whole entire community."

"All I know is that I can't be a part of what I saw today. And whatever we're doing—if it's in any way connected to that whole thing—then I can't be involved in that either."

"Oh, so now you're breaking up our celibate 'spiritual friendship' because you're triggered by a few guys in leather?"

We sat next to each other in silence for several minutes as tears rolled down Amelia's cheeks. Then we had an official "spiritual friendship breakup" dinner at a pizza place in Berkeley. The next morning, we headed to the airport to fly our separate ways. When we hugged each other goodbye, we knew it was the end of our experiment.

I had taken all the shame and fear I felt about inhabiting a lesbian body and turned it into a shield to keep Amelia away. What had she done to deserve it? She had loved me too much.

That weekend in San Francisco was part of a larger pattern in my movement away from fundamentalism. I would inch toward acceptance and start to feel new parts of myself waking up to life. Then I would slink back in fear, doubling down on the belief that celebrating same-sex love was active participation in sin.

The weekend had been a trial run for me. Ultimately, I wasn't ready to see the queer community in all of its complexity, with a wide range of experiences and expressions, like any other community. My eyes weren't open to the resilience and grace that radiated from thousands of marchers.

When I reflect on that weekend now, I remember a pale, skinny man in his late fifties or early sixties, strolling alone in the parade, wearing knee-length khaki shorts, a faded blue T-shirt, and a baseball cap. He unironically wore wire-rimmed glasses straight out of the 1960s. He looked like a dad who spent the bulk of his paycheck on his family, ensuring they had the food they needed and the clothes they wanted. This solo walker caught my attention because when he walked by my section and scanned the crowd, he bit his lip and squinted as he raised a fist in the air, as if his whole life had been building up to this moment, and still it surpassed his expectations.

His face told a story of grief turned to gratitude and ultimately triumph, of someone who had endured great loss and yet survived to see this: thousands of people throwing a party for people like him. This man, who I can only imagine was picked on, bullied, and beat up as a middle schooler, who might have married a woman in an attempt to pass, who surely saw loved ones die brutal and lonely deaths in the AIDS crisis, was an occasion for celebration that day. People lined the streets, climbed up fences, and jumped on partners' backs to get a better view of the show in which he starred. He might have grown up in a world that wanted him straight or dead, but he survived to see a day when crowds cheered for queers like him.

9

The week after I returned from Pride in San Francisco, Wheaton College invited me to go through a second round of interviews for a job as an associate chaplain. Ten years earlier, I had a brief stint as a student at Wheaton. My mom's conservative Evangelical friends referred to it as the "Harvard of Christian schools," so she sent VHS tapes of my high school basketball games to the women's coach and asked her to call me for an interview. After a few phone calls and a campus visit, my mom was sold. I moved into a room in Smith Hall that September and started my new life at a school that was not created for queer students. By the middle of the fall semester, I was so depressed that I failed fitness class and had to sit out the second half of the basketball season. Eleven a.m. is too early to get out of bed for class when you're a depressed, repressed, queer student at an Evangelical college.

So when the associate chaplain who oversaw Wheaton's support group for LGBTQ students invited me to apply for a new job in the chaplain's office, I was intrigued. Part of the job would be to meet with all kinds of students who needed a safe person to talk to outside of the counseling center. The other part of the role would be to support LGBTQ students and lead Refuge, the queer student group. Clayton, the chaplain who reached out to me, was a sensitive and compassionate straight man. After a few years of listening to LGBTQ students, he understood they needed a queer role model, someone they could look up to, who truly empathized with them and had their backs.

The challenge was that this person also needed to be able to sign Wheaton's Statement of Faith, which said that marriage is reserved for one man and one woman and that sex is only permissible in that context. Essentially, they needed a queer person who was committed to remaining single and celibate, who would affirm a traditional view of marriage, and who could also connect with both progressive students and conservative administrators. According to Clayton, they needed someone just like me.

On the first Tuesday of the fall semester, more than twenty students squished into a living room at an apartment across the street from the college. The place smelled like chocolate because Jacob, one of the seniors, had baked a cake to welcome everyone back. The living room was loud and stuffy. As each new student burst through the door, the group erupted into cheers and rushed to squeeze one another. Even when they settled into conversations, they shouted their stories. They laughed and squealed and hung their arms around each other's necks over the course of entire conversations. It was the first Refuge meeting of the year. They were finally reunited with their queer family.

"Um, hi, everyone!" a petite student in jeans and a navy sweater yelled after about ten minutes of mingling. "It's so great to see you all! For those of you who don't know me, I'm Bradley, and this is my apartment."

Bradley had a deep, raspy voice, and he ended most sentences at a higher pitch, like he was asking a question.

"I'm so excited to be hosting Refuge this year!" he said, clasping his hands. "I collected cute mugs all summer long so I would have enough for everyone to have tea on Tuesdays, so just help yourself. Also, Jacob was super sweet to bake a cake for everyone tonight, so let's all thank Jacob!"

A tall, fair-skinned guy in an apron waved from the kitchen and smiled as everyone cheered.

"We're gonna get started soon," Bradley continued. "Get some cake and ice cream, and then let's see how many people we can fit on these couches!"

The room was clearly designed with Refuge in mind: there were two large sofas, one white and one gray, with a navy-blue love seat in between them, forming a rectangle. Students sat four or five to a couch, with some guys resting their arms around other's shoulders. Two students squeezed into a brown leather chair made for one in the corner. Others took seats on the floor and leaned back against couches, comfortably nestled between friends' legs.

After another minute of chatter, Clayton, my colleague in the chaplain's office, spoke up.

"Well, welcome back, everyone. We have quite a bit to cover tonight, but before we get going, I want to introduce Julie Rodgers, who is joining us in the chaplain's office this year. I know many of you are already familiar with her work, and I'll let her share more about herself, but I just want to say quickly that I'm thrilled to have Julie joining our team. I think you all are going to love her."

I felt the gaze of the whole circle upon me as I opened my mouth into a wide, enthusiastic smile. It felt like my first day of school.

"Since she's new here, why don't we all go around and introduce ourselves?" Clayton continued.

More than twenty students each took a minute to let their personalities shine. Christopher, a senior political science major with bright-blue eyes and a preppy style, was one of the ringleaders. "Hiiiiii! I'm Christopher," he started. "I'm a senior and one of the founding members of Refuge. I was a part of forming this community with a few other queer folks who have since graduated, and it's so exciting to see how it's grown."

"Hi, everyone. I'm James," a Black student with thick, black, rectangular glasses spoke up. James was the youngest in the group, and students around the circle collectively said "Aww" after he spoke, as if he was their nephew.

"Isn't James just *adorable*?" Christopher said from across the room.

"Hi, I'm Evelyn," a soft-spoken girl with a denim jacket and black boots spoke up. "I'm a senior anthropology major, and, um, I spent the summer in Georgia with my family."

It was a diverse group in terms of personalities, interests, and styles. There were two Black students and one Asian American student—the other twenty or so were white. There were a few women, but the group was mostly made up of guys. No freshmen were involved yet because it was only the second day of school, so a freshman wouldn't have had the chance to go through an intake interview with someone from the chaplain's office, which students had to do to attend Refuge. Since most of the students came from conservative Christian families, it took many of them a while to feel safe enough to come out even to themselves, much less other people.

Once we had made our way around the circle, everyone turned their gaze to me.

"Well, for those of you I haven't had the chance to meet yet, I'm Julie!" I felt sweat seeping through my soft, light-green oxford button-up. "This is my second day on staff in the chaplain's office, and my whole entire purpose in this role is just to support you all and to be available to meet with students who need to process questions and fears and all the feelings. First, I want to say that you are my priority, and I would love to get a meal or coffee with every single one of you and just get to know you. I can already tell this is an extraordinary crew, and we're going to adore each other."

Students around the circle smiled and nodded, excited to be in the room with someone on staff who was noticeably gay.

Christopher filled the brief silence: "Um, can I just say your shoe game is, like, totally on point?"

"Ha, thank you, thank you," I said, uncomfortable with the natural process of evaluation. Students were deliberating within themselves, deciding if I was gay enough—if I seemed relatable, approachable, trustworthy.

"A little about me: you may or may not know, I'm gay!"

"Hey girl!" someone yelled. People whooped and hollered.

"Like many of you, I come from a conservative Christian family—my mom actually homeschooled me all the way until high school to keep me away from the gays and science teachers. But I didn't do any school. My brother and I watched *Matlock* every morning at 10:05 and we watched four episodes of *Saved by the Bell* every afternoon. If any of you saw it, Kelly Kapowski was my first crush!"

Half the room laughed, and half didn't catch the reference. The show ended before any of the students were born.

"Anyway, I came out to my mom on Valentine's Day of my junior year in high school, and a week later, she took me to a ministry called Living Hope, a member ministry of Exodus International, which was the largest organization in the world that proclaimed 'freedom from homosexuality through Jesus Christ.'" I made quotation marks in the air with my fingers and everyone joined me in a collective eye roll.

"I spent almost a decade in that movement and then realized I was still super gay! For the last few years," I continued, "I've been trying to figure out what it means to be gay in communities that have traditional views of marriage. I honestly love Jesus. I love that he always moved toward the kinds of people others push away."

I scanned the room, trying to gauge the interest in a conversation about Jesus. Some looked me in the eye, eager to hear more. Others stared at the ground, likely exhausted by a religion that hadn't, at any point, had good news for people like them.

"We are the first generation of queer people to be out in the Evangelical church," I continued. "In the speaking and writing I do, I try to help straight Christians become more compassionate. I want them to understand we didn't choose this, and we can't change it. I want them to know they actually need us—that we have gifts to offer the church, not in spite of the fact that we're queer, but because of it. And yeah, I'm trying to figure out, for me, what long-term celibacy might look like—how I can create a chosen family if the church isn't going to allow me to marry and gain a family through the traditional structures available. I have friends all over the spectrum in terms of theology: some who date and marry people of the same sex and some who are pursuing celibacy like me, but I feel like we're all on the same team. My goal is to create more hospitable communities for queer people in the church, regardless of where we land in terms of theology and relationships. All of that to say, I'm pumped to be here and can't wait to get to know each of you, so email me and let's hang!"

The extroverts broke into chatter immediately. A student next to me asked for my email address to connect about getting lunch that week.

"Okay, everyone!" Clayton interrupted. "Before we head out, a few quick things." He ran through some announcements, and then cleared his throat and said, "Now it's time for the most important thing."

A student next to me whispered, "Oh my God, prepare yourself."

Clayton looked around the room. Moving his big blue eyes slowly around the circle so he could gaze directly into each of our eyes, he pronounced this blessing over the group: "Remember this: God loves you more than you could ever imagine. He loves you with a love that has no beginning and no end. It is a love you don't have to earn and you could never lose. Whether you feel like a success or a failure, he loves you. Whether you feel alone or surrounded by people, he loves you. Whether you feel righteous or guilty, he loves you. He loves you enough to send his Son to live for you, to die for you, and be raised for you. Even right now, Jesus is before the Father, speaking words of love on your behalf. He will return to renew you and the whole world because he loves you. This is the most true thing about you. This is the first fact of your existence: you are loved by God. Before anything else can be said about you, this must be said: God loves you, and that will never change. So don't forget it. Go in peace."

I felt a knot in my throat. As I scanned the room, I saw tears in students' eyes. They had heard generic statements about God's love before, but they never heard it said specifically to them in contexts where they were known to be gay. Clayton's pronouncement of unconditional love visibly shook them.

With that, the meeting was over. I walked outside with Clayton and Marissa, Refuge's other sponsor.

"Man, that was amazing!" I said the moment we were alone. "I've never been in a Christian setting where a bunch of gays felt so free to let their guards down and still feel surrounded by the love of Jesus."

"I thought your introduction was perfect," Clayton said as we walked together in the crisp, early-September air.

"I couldn't agree more!" Marissa chimed in. "I just feel like God handpicked you for this position and that you are exactly the leader Refuge needs right now."

It was the rare kind of night when all the events of my life made sense. All the fears, failures, and insecurities I carried throughout my life were worth it if they prepared me for this: being an openly gay chaplain at an Evangelical college where I could hold sacred space for queer students to tell the truth about themselves.

I wanted to somehow seal the moment in my memory, to capture the scene and put it in a snow globe so I would never forget what it felt like to know that the things that had disqualified me in countless situations were assets in this role. I wasn't an embarrassment. I wasn't a freak. I was actually an expert, a role model, a perfect fit for an important position that made a tangible difference in the lives of people who mattered. *It's gotta be too good to be true*, I marveled to myself as I drove out of the parking lot. *I wonder when the other shoe will drop.*

10

On the Friday of my first week at Wheaton, President Ryken approached me on my way to chapel and asked, "Julie, could I have a word with you?"

I followed him to the side of the room and noticed, for the first time that year, how small I was. Or maybe he was tall? At well over six feet, he towered over me. The top of my head barely reached his shoulder.

"I hope your move went as smoothly as possible," he started.

"Yeah, my first week here has been such a joy!" I said enthusiastically.

"Good. Good," he replied, not matching my cheer. "Listen, I wanted to alert you to some feedback I received from constituents this week about your presence on social media. Apparently, you tweeted that an article was 'amazing,' and that article was written by someone who's in a homosexual relationship."

"Um, yeah, I think I retweeted an article by a lesbian who's married to a woman, but the article wasn't about same-sex marriage. It was about tokenism and feeling pressure to be perfect around straight Christians, as if they're always watching and making judgments about the whole LGBTQ community based on her every move."

"Yes, I read the article you linked to," he replied. "I wouldn't say it was 'amazing,' but I understand your point."

"Well, I actually didn't say it was amazing—I just retweeted someone else who did. Honestly, I didn't put a lot of thought into it. I was just intrigued by it and wanted people to consider her point." I shifted my weight from one foot to the other and scanned the room, noticing it was empty and totally quiet.

President Ryken continued: "One aspect of this job that might be an adjustment for you is understanding that when you share your personal views about something, it can be interpreted by some as you speaking on behalf of Wheaton College. Obviously, you and I know the difference between something you share from your personal account and an official statement from the college, but other people don't always make that distinction. For better or worse, Wheaton is often looked to as a leader in evangelicalism, and I think a lot of people are wondering where we stand on the issue of homosexuality in light of your hire. Unfortunately, there's a bit of a spotlight on Wheaton College and now on you as a result of the nature of your position."

"Yeah, that makes sense," I conceded, crossing my arms and putting my hand over my mouth as I reflected.

"I'm confident we'll figure this out," he said after a brief silence. "We're obviously in uncharted territory with your new role, and there will be challenges that come up along the way that we might have to navigate together. I mainly just wanted to make you aware of this tension so you can consider the implications of things you share from your personal social media pages."

"Thanks for the heads-up," I said, scanning the room for some sort of escape, a restroom, anything.

My chest felt tight. I'm sure he thought it was a casual conversation—just an FYI to a new staff member to help me adjust. But I felt his power in my body. He was the president of the college, and I was a lower-level staff member. He was twice my size. And I knew from his books and speeches that he believed men were appointed by God to be the authority in the church and the home. I felt small in his presence. I understood I was being watched by people who reported back to him.

Not even a week into my new role, it was clear that my body was seen as scandalous in some Wheaton circles.

My office was already a hot spot, with students cycling in and out every hour. My job was to listen to them like a therapist and offer guidance like a minister. After about a week into the job, my schedule was full of students wanting to process. Some were queer, and they wanted to tell me their stories. They had questions about theology and coming out to family members. They wanted to know if it was possible to be happy someday as an openly queer person in Christian communities. Sometimes students stopped by in groups unannounced to gossip or tell me about their weekends. Sometimes they came alone and sat quietly, staring at the floor while they tried to find words to tell the truth about themselves to another human for the first time, just like I had done in Turner's office years earlier.

Another group of students I met with were straight ones who had heard about "the new gay chaplain." During the first round of these meetings, I met with people who thought it was awesome that Wheaton was finally catching up with the twenty-first century. Maybe they had gay roommates or bisexual best friends. Of course you could be gay and Christian, they said.

They were graduating into a world that thought Evangelicals were crazy for having so much anxiety about queer people. They wanted to see me in the flesh and tell me how much they loved their gay friends.

Over time, these students started to bring their problems to me too. Some were Black and frustrated by the ignorance of their white peers. Others wanted to talk about their eating disorders and thought the gay chaplain might be a safe person to process their body image issues with. All kinds of students began to find refuge in my office. They brought their doubts, their questions, their struggles with self-harm and mental health, and they poured them out to the one person who, by nature of being in a body that was often misunderstood and maligned, would sympathize with them in their suffering.

I also met with staff and faculty who came with a range of motives. Some knew what I was up against with the administration, and they wanted to support me. Others didn't know what to make of me, and they wanted to get a pulse. Then there were those who knew LGBTQ issues were at the heart of the drama at Wheaton and just wanted gossip. While I was happy to answer the range of questions that came from staff and faculty, I had my own agenda.

After my meeting with President Ryken during my first week on the job, I knew I needed to do my own research. Whenever staff or faculty said something like "I'm sure you're already learning that Wheaton can be a challenging place to navigate" or "People in leadership here tend to be fearful of change," I took it as a sign. I would tell a select few, especially if they had already been vetted by queer students, that I didn't know what I had gotten into at Wheaton and I needed to

understand the lay of the land. In almost all of these meetings, whether with students or faculty, at some point in the
conversation they brought up Stan Jones.

Dr. Stanton Jones was in his nineteenth year as provost of
Wheaton when I was hired, after already serving as the chair
of the psychology department for fourteen years. One of
Wheaton's most prominent voices, Stan had written more than
a dozen books and published more than eighty-five scholarly
and popular articles. He was best known for his research on
human sexuality, particularly on the question of whether gay
people could become straight.

His work set the tone for conversations about LGBTQ
issues at Wheaton, and his research and lectures implied that
he believed the most biblical response to queer people was to
pursue "healing" from their same-sex attractions. If someone
couldn't succeed in that effort, they were challenged to perse-
vere nonetheless, disidentifying from everything related to a
queer identity and living a chaste life until death.

Stan became a significant figure in the battle between
Evangelicals and the LGBTQ community. People on both
sides used his words to create caricatures that preceded him.
By the queer community, he was vilified; by conservatives, he
was acclaimed; and by faculty, staff, and students at Wheaton,
he was feared.

Stan was on vacation when I interviewed at Wheaton, and
I didn't do enough research before I took the job. Since openly
queer students called for support for same-sex marriage on
the internet, I assumed that Wheaton was pretty progressive
for an Evangelical institution. I thought it was strange that I
had a one-on-one interview with President Ryken in his office,

where he told me about several people that he helped "leave the homosexual lifestyle" when he was a pastor in Philadelphia, but everyone else I spoke with that day made me feel like I would be right at home at Wheaton as an out lesbian.

It wasn't until I had moved a thousand miles away from my home in Texas that I understood the internal battle for Wheaton College's identity and image—and that LGBTQ issues were at the center of the conflict.

o o o

I first heard about the LGBTQ dialogue from an email making the rounds through the administration. Apparently, Christopher created a Facebook event that morning for a student-led dialogue to take place later that afternoon called "LGBTQ at Wheaton." It was mid-November, and I had been in the chaplaincy role for almost three months, so I was aware of some of the tensions.

Christopher's impromptu gathering ruffled feathers among administrators. A senior political science major, Christopher took every opportunity to let people know he had been a founding member of Refuge. He had a charm that often felt forced, as if it were masking a sense of rage boiling just beneath the surface. He didn't trust anyone in Wheaton's administration, so he naturally didn't trust me because Wheaton had hired me. He had been betrayed too many times by Christians.

Christopher understood how systems operated, and while he knew the administration had the power to put him on probation or kick him out, he also knew media could be weaponized for protection. He had connections with journalists, and he was savvy on social media. He knew that Wheaton cared about optics and that bad press hurt their image. In his final year at Wheaton, Christopher seemed eager to leave his mark as the out, proud, empowered queer student who defied authority in his fight for liberation.

He also had important institutional knowledge that I couldn't get from staffers or administrators. Where administrators often filtered things through a lens that reflected positively on themselves, Christopher's reports gave me insight into how things affected students—particularly queer ones and vulnerable ones.

In the hours leading up to the event, administrators fired emails back and forth, deliberating about how to proceed. If they let the dialogue happen, Christopher would have direct access to the student body, and they feared he would attempt to convince conservative students that the Bible doesn't condemn same-sex relationships. The college worked hard to ensure students were not exposed to arguments that fully affirmed queer students. But if administrators shut the event down altogether, they would appear to be stifling the conversation.

Wheaton was a liberal arts institution, after all. They presented a public face of being open to engaging in difficult conversations, supposedly believing the truth can stand for itself when it's interrogated.

At some point during the process of deliberation, I finally asked, "Can someone help me understand what rule Christopher technically violated? On what grounds could this event be shut down?"

I was told he didn't reserve the room where the dialogue was set to take place.

"Wait, what?" I said to no one in particular. "This is the student center. Students gather everywhere. At what size is a study group supposed to formally book a room?"

The response I got was that Christopher knew if he had gone through the proper channels to book the room, a larger conversation about the nature of the dialogue would have ensued. Some administrators expressed fear that this was his attempt to start an informal Gay–Straight Alliance on campus.

Despite my concerns, I was inclined to side with the administration. In Refuge meetings, I sometimes sensed that Christopher tried to assert dominance. He might show up with guided conversation topics when he knew I had prepared remarks. Sometimes he brought new students to Refuge meetings when they hadn't done intake interviews with chaplain staff. It wasn't hard to believe administrators who feared this was some sort of power play.

By early afternoon, the administration decided not to interfere with the event. They also decided I would attend the dialogue. The higher-ups thought that was the best compromise—they wouldn't have to stomp out discussions about LGBTQ issues, but they could still have a staff presence at the meeting (and, therefore, ears on the ground) without the appearance of straight folks imposing.

At 3:00 that afternoon, more than fifty students gathered in a large room in the student center, and I casually slid into a seat close to the exit, intent on saying as little as possible.

Christopher had a commanding presence. With his legs crossed and head held high, he addressed the room: "Welcome, everyone! My name is Christopher, and I'm one of the cofounders of Refuge, a community for LGBTQ students here at Wheaton College. On behalf of my fellow queer students, both out and closeted, I want to thank you for making time on such short notice to come learn about our experiences here at Wheaton."

The room was packed. Everyone sat at attention. Students were eager to hear from their queer classmates.

For a little over an hour, LGBTQ students fielded questions from their straight peers on topics like terminology and how they could help make Wheaton a safer place for queer students. A couple of people asked questions that revealed they had conservative views on same-sex relationships, and the conversation was civil and productive. Christopher made it a point to steer clear of theology, instead choosing to emphasize goals they shared, like ensuring that all students felt safe and loved.

The conversation was far from the explosive and coercive agenda the administration feared. In fact, the only time someone argued for an affirming view of same-sex relationships was when a straight student passionately thanked the queer students in the room for their courage and vulnerability. In a statement of repentance on behalf of her peers, she lamented the homophobic conditions of the college and pleaded with her straight classmates to reconsider their views on same-sex relationships.

That was it. That was the extent of advocacy for affirming theology.

After the dialogue, I returned to my office to spend some time in reflection. All queer students wanted was an opportunity to share honestly with their straight peers. If more than sixty people cleared their afternoon schedules with just a few·

hours' notice to attend a dialogue about LGBTQ issues, then there was obviously a hunger for these kinds of conversations among the broader student body.

Why had I been so quick to assume the worst about Christopher's motives and the best about the administration? After everything I had already witnessed from Evangelicals in power, why did I still want to distance myself from the queer community and align with the administration? Why didn't I give queer folks the benefit of the doubt?

11

Gabe Lyons was thrilled that Wheaton had hired me. Maybe he saw me as the solution to the problem Evangelicals faced: if they embraced celibate gay Christians, then they couldn't be accused of discriminating based on sexual orientation when they denied rights to people in same-sex relationships. I was proof that their dissent was about theological beliefs, not anti-gay animus.

Otherwise, a prominent Evangelical college wouldn't hire me, and megachurches wouldn't invite me to speak in their churches. Gabe gave me a bigger platform, and by promoting me at conferences like Q, Evangelical pastors, college administrators, and key stakeholders could see this was the new plan. Conservative gay Christians could lead them to a victory in the culture war.

In a phone call from my new office, Gabe and I discussed my upcoming keynote at the inaugural Q Women's conference.

"I really want to make the point that if Christians are going to insist that gay people commit to never date or marry, then the church is going to have to become family to the LGBTQ people in their lives," I said to Gabe. "I mean, think about it: we need people to text when we make it to our destination on a road trip, and we need a family to unwind with on Tuesday nights at the end of a hard day at work. I want Christians to understand that their beliefs about what gay people should do with their whole entire relational future should cost *them* something too. The burden of their beliefs can't entirely rest on gay people."

"Mmm, that's good stuff," Gabe replied. "So important. I want to also make sure you really emphasize the importance of the church holding to the orthodox, historic view of marriage."

"Yeah, I'm going to be clear about what I believe," I told him. "It's just not my main point."

Gabe said we were facing a watershed moment in the church as people were exposed to gay Christian activists like Matthew Vines, who made a biblical argument that said Christians can celebrate their friends in same-sex relationships.

"I think that's the real power of your story," Gabe continued. "You're saying, 'Yeah I feel these desires just as strongly as any gay person you know, but I'm choosing costly obedience because of my allegiance to Christ.' People need to hear testimonies of that kind of faithfulness."

I tried to shift the focus back to my hope for the session, which was to help straight Christians understand that gay Christians exist and that the church has caused a lot of suffering for LGBTQ people.

"For sure, that's good stuff," he responded. "I don't think it's an either/or. You can and should emphasize those points. I also recognize the power of a firm call for Christians to hold fast to orthodox teaching on marriage and sexuality coming from you specifically. If I stand up and say gay people need to be celibate if they want to be faithful, I sound like a bigot because I'm a straight, white man. It has a lot more power coming from you."

"I get it," I said finally. "I'll be sure to emphasize the importance of holding on to traditional views of marriage. I'm just so thankful you're willing to have these hard conversations at Q, and I'm grateful to be a part of it."

After the call ended, I leaned back in my office chair with my hands on top of my head and took a deep breath. That was the first time I had heard a straight Christian leader explicitly say he needed a queer person to make the argument against same-sex relationships so that he wouldn't sound like a bigot. The ex-gay leaders I had worked with had been manipulative too, but almost all of them said they "struggled with same-sex attractions" themselves. In their own way, they admitted they were gay. While they benefited from their teaching, they also bore the consequences of it in various ways. It was alarming to hear a straight Evangelical leader say he needed me to shield him from accusations of homophobia. Up until then, I felt thankful and unworthy when Evangelical leaders invited me into their circles. This was the first time I wondered if I was being used.

Meanwhile, at Wheaton, President Ryken asked me to write a personal statement about my theology and approach to ministry. "We continue to receive a steady stream—anywhere from a trickle to a flood—of emails about your hire," President Ryken said to me in a meeting. "How is your personal statement coming along?"

In a one- to two-page statement, he wanted me to explain my choice to identify as "gay." He explained that it created confusion for a lot of people. The concern, I was told, was that my use of the term *gay* might suggest I was open to same-sex relationships. Some Evangelicals also believed it was a sinful identity; they thought I should find my identity "in Christ" rather than my sexuality. President Ryken thought it would be helpful to have a personal statement from me that he could send to critics.

I agreed to write it and refrained from asking if other staff members had to write personal statements defending their humanity.

Wheaton's director of media relations and President Ryken relayed their sense of urgency about the statement because the conservative journalist Julie Roys planned to write an article critical of me for the prominent Evangelical publication *WORLD* magazine.

By early December, Stan Jones and President Ryken were deeply involved in the editing process. Evidently, I was mistaken to assume a personal statement would reflect my views rather than theirs. Several meetings and countless emails focused on one critical issue: they wanted me to say I was open to "healing" and marrying a man if God were to change me.

I was not open to marrying a man. I didn't think my gay orientation was something that needed to be healed. In fact, I thought it was a gift, a blessing, and an expression of the kind of diversity we see in all of creation.

After trying (and failing) to persuade me to write something that mirrored their perspective, they opted to rewrite entire paragraphs for me. I incorporated as many of their suggestions as I could but told them I absolutely would not say I was open to marrying a man. I reminded them how harmful the message of "change" and "healing" was for queer Christians who absolutely would not change.

After much back-and-forth, the final statement had a qualifying phrase where I said I was "open to God's sanctifying work in my life." It was vague enough for people to read into it whatever they wanted. I needed the damn thing to be done.

Months later, I learned that the Senior Administrative Cabinet (SAC) planned to put my personal statement on Wheaton's website when LaTonya Taylor, director of media relations, called a meeting, bringing the director of human resources to let them know it was inappropriate to single out one employee on their website with a statement about her sexual orientation. The five white men who made up SAC at that time listened to LaTonya and decided to go with the original plan to send my personal statement to people on an individual basis when faced with questions or criticism, which, President Ryken often reminded me, was frequent.

The *WORLD* magazine article went live at noon on a Thursday, and the internet was soon engulfed in an all-out war over my presence at Wheaton. Conservative Christians were outraged that Wheaton had hired someone who openly identified as gay and believed there were ways in which a gay orientation could be a gift. Progressives, despite being skeptical of me because of my traditional values, came to my defense, angry that Evangelicals couldn't even accept a *celibate* lesbian who shared their views on sex and marriage.

As the battle raged, I headed home to my apartment in a neighboring town and fell into bed. It was already dark. It was cold. I lived alone in a basement with a tiny window near the ceiling. I wanted to talk to someone about my week—about the onslaught of emails from the administration, the pushback

I got from within Wheaton and without, Julie Roys's hit job, and the internet's battle over my lesbian body.

I wanted someone to acknowledge how shitty it was for people to debate about LGBTQ people as if it were a sport. I wanted to tell someone about the student who broke out in hives when he came out to me in my office weeks earlier—how he stuttered and apologized for the red spots crawling up his neck, reassuring me that he was okay, saying this sometimes happened when he got really anxious.

But no one was there to bear witness to my actual human life in my cold, dark basement apartment. I was a liability or a threat—to some, a sign of hope—anything but a human being.

o o o

Christmas break did not bring the relief I longed for as my first semester at Wheaton came to a close. My mom was still very unhappy that I was gay.

"I got a thank-you card from Ricky a few days ago," she told me, "because I gave $1,000 to Living Hope on Giving Tuesday. He's always so sweet about making sure to thank me when I give, and I give a lot to them. They need support now more than ever."

I pretended to watch the holiday movie playing on my mom's TV.

"What does Ricky think about your choice to identify as gay?" she asked, as if we hadn't already exhausted the topic.

"We've talked about this, and you know he disagrees with it. Ricky and I are obviously in different places, but he understands there's absolutely no biblical argument against my choice to be honest about my orientation as I live a single and celibate life."

"Well, I still don't understand why you are placing your identity in your sin instead of Christ." She couldn't help herself.

"You tell people you're straight, don't you?" I said, annoyed. "Do you feel like you're 'finding your identity in your sexuality rather than Christ'?"

"I'm sorry that I want you to have a husband who sweeps you off your feet and protects you and takes care of you!" She was crying. "I just want God's best for you, and I know that homosexuality is not it."

"I'm not having this conversation again," I said, calm and cold. "You're going to have to work through your feelings about my sexuality with someone other than me."

I finally understood I was not responsible for my mom's mental and emotional health. For years, I believed that if I could fix my sexuality—become straight or at least remain single and celibate—then she would be happy. By this point, I understood that her refusal to accept her daughter was her problem, and she alone could fix it.

"Listen," I said to her months earlier in a call. "You have a lesbian daughter. You do not have a straight daughter. You can either have a relationship with your actual daughter, or you will miss out on a relationship with me because of your unwillingness to acknowledge the reality that I am, and always will be, a lesbian. I can't make that decision for you."

My short trip home for Christmas gave me no reason to believe she was moving toward acceptance.

On Christmas Eve, my whole family met up at my brother Michael's church for a candlelit service. By that point, both of my brothers had graduated from Texas A&M University and married women who went to Baylor University. They both had jobs at big banks in suburbs north of Dallas. They both had kids—Michael had three and Kenny had two—and their families were active members in conservative Evangelical megachurches.

I was politically progressive, a feminist, a lesbian. Even though I was doing everything I could to keep my place in Evangelical circles, I clearly didn't fit. I physically felt their discomfort once I was out as a celibate lesbian. We had the unspoken agreement made between many conservative Evangelicals and their mostly estranged LGBTQ loved ones: I could hang around as long as I didn't verbalize my differences. The moment my queerness became evident, the deal was off.

We all performed our way through Christmas, focusing our attention on the kids and their new toys with forced enthusiasm. Michael and I never revisited the conversation we had when I was in high school—the one where he said he hoped I didn't choose to be gay because he wanted me to be able to come around his kids. I understood the need to abide by our unspoken agreement and that, even then, I was on thin ice.

Before leaving Dallas to return to Wheaton for the spring semester, I saw Ricky for what would be the last time. We met for coffee at a Starbucks, a sign that our relationship had changed from the days when I left family holidays early to end them at his home. I told Ricky about the challenges I faced at Wheaton: the criticism from conservative constituents, the pressure from the administration, the suffering among queer students, the loneliness of being an experiment for Evangelicals.

I longed for him to empathize, to tell me in his deep, sooth-ing voice that I was doing the Lord's work and he was proud of me. But Ricky agreed with Wheaton's conservative constitu-ents: he thought I was walking a dangerous line by referring to myself as "gay" and highlighting the gifts queer people bring to the church. He listened. He was cordial. Ultimately, though, he said he was afraid I had given up on healing. He worried I was on a slippery slope.

The problem with the "slippery slope" analogy is that it implies we're at the top of the mountain. My friend Peter Choi, a historian and pastor, notes that the analogy assumes we have the truth, the moral high ground, and that any shift toward a different perspective is downward movement. The metaphor doesn't leave much room for humility, where we consider the possibility that people with different perspectives might be right about some things and we might be wrong or that we might both be a little right, in different ways. I needed a framework that accounted for the ways we might be wrong, especially after bearing witness to the suffering queer people experienced in Christian communities.

Ricky updated me on his life: Living Hope was thriving. He was speaking in megachurches, at prominent seminaries, in Canada, in Germany, in Australia. More than one hundred people attended group meetings most Thursday nights, and more than five thousand people were on their online forums. He continued to face criticism from the culture, but he said God was faith-ful to him, and his ministry was gaining more and more momentum.

Ricky seemed reserved and distant that day. Part of me was thankful we had settled into a place of respect amid our

disagreements, but the other part of me longed to feel like
he was more emotionally invested. I didn't want constant dis-
agreement, but indifference felt worse from someone who
had been like a father to me. When we hugged in the parking
lot before parting ways, I didn't know he had reached the end
of his journey with me—that when he released me from that
hug, he was letting go of me for good.

o o o

Despite the difficulties of my first semester at Wheaton, I was
relieved to return to Chicago after Christmas. The pushback
about my sexuality at Wheaton was at least an acknowledgment that I existed: I was an out lesbian who was a leader at
an Evangelical institution, a consultant for Christian colleges
around the country, and a keynote speaker at Evangelical conferences. While the controversy around my presence made me
anxious, I preferred that anxiety to the torment of having to
hide to belong in my circles in Texas. Since my family didn't
want to hear about my queerness, no one asked me questions
about my life for fear of what the answers might hold. I was
in my late twenties, and my family never asked whether I dated
or what I imagined for my relational future. I felt invisible and
unknown, and you can't be loved when you aren't known.

I celebrated New Year's Eve with some friends from the
gay Christian blogosphere, and the next day I moved from
the basement apartment near Wheaton to Oak Park, a more
diverse city. From my apartment in Oak Park, I could walk one
block to catch a train that dropped me in downtown Chicago
in twenty minutes or take the Metra for a thirty-minute train
ride west to Wheaton.

The distance from Wheaton gave me space to exhale. In Wheaton, I felt the anxiety of being "the gay chaplain" in my body. When I visited churches, eyes widened when members shook my hand: "Oh, you're the new chaplain! I've heard so much about you!" I didn't like the feeling of being talked about, the feeling of being watched. I wanted to be known.

Oak Park was a place where I could be known. A handful of Wheaton professors lived there because they also needed some distance from the college. Most of them were Black or Brown, and they were among the only nonwhite faculty members. Four of them shared monthly dinners in one another's homes, and they often commuted to work together on the train.

I was invited to attend my first dinner late in the fall semester at the invitation of Ezer Kang, a psychology professor at Wheaton. Ezer spent Thursdays seeing patients at a clinic in Lawndale, most of whom were men living with HIV. He and his wife and two daughters attended a small Black Episcopal church in Oak Park as well, where the priest was an openly gay man. When Ezer and I met, he immediately saw how vulnerable I was, and he said he wanted to introduce me to his friends in Oak Park.

A few weeks later, I found myself at a table with Ezer, his wife and two daughters, and a handful of other professors. Larycia Hawkins, a popular professor of political science, was the first Black woman to receive tenure in Wheaton's history. Larycia was adored by students. She knew what it felt like to walk across campus in a body that was the subject of scrutiny in white Evangelical spaces, which made her a safe place for all kinds of marginalized students. She challenged the Wheaton community to follow in the footsteps of Jesus, who stood with and for the oppressed.

Christine Folch was another popular professor at Wheaton. An anthropologist who was raised in a bilingual household by immigrant parents, Christine challenged students to think not just about individual choices but about systems and power structures, how they functioned, who they protected, and who they exploited. There was a handful of other regulars at Oak Park dinners, and there were always open seats for people who needed a place to belong.

As soon as I met them, I felt seen. I didn't have to tell them about the personal statement, the *WORLD* magazine article, or the private conversations with President Ryken for them to know I wasn't well.

The decision to move to Oak Park changed my life. I suddenly had a family, and that family comprised people who understood the power dynamics at play in my job even better than I did. More than the sense of solidarity I felt in this community of minorities, their friendship was profoundly healing to me. They all had deeply pastoral sensibilities. They were empathetic and nurturing. They also came from conservative Christian backgrounds and still loved Jesus. In their own ways, they wrestled with questions similar to the ones I faced. We were grappling with what it meant to follow Jesus in the twenty-first century, which we all believed meant prioritizing the poor, the vulnerable, the oppressed.

Several times a week, toward the end of our workdays, we texted each other to see which train the others were catching and then made the half-mile walk through the snow to commute home together. Sometimes that led to happy hours back in Oak Park, where we didn't have to live in fear of people watching us or listening in on our conversations. We could be Black or Brown or queer or progressive and absolutely no one cared. Oak Park became the place where a sisterhood grew, and while I didn't know it when I made the move, that sisterhood would eventually save my life.

o o o

President Ryken's office door opened, and he motioned for me to come inside.

I took a seat in a large, dark-green velvet chair near a window, and he sat down in a matching chair to my left, with a coffee table serving as a buffer between us. With his legs crossed and a notepad on his lap, he got straight to the point: "I continue to hear positive things about your work on campus and understand your ministry with students is very fruitful."

"Thanks for that encouragement," I said, hoping the new semester would be an opportunity for a fresh start.

"The difficulty for us is that, as we've discussed many times now, we continue to receive a lot of criticism about your appointment from constituents, particularly in the offices of admissions and advancement. I've shared some of the nature of that criticism with you, but that's just a small sample."

"I'm well aware of the criticism," I said, wondering why we were rehashing this again. "Like I've said before, conservative critics aren't going to listen to anything I have to say. You're the one who can influence them by showing public support for me."

"I think we would be wise to consider our options moving forward," he said dryly, as if he hadn't heard my plea for public support. "Because of the toll your presence is taking on the college, I could foresee a situation in which you might choose to resign."

After a pause, I asked, "What exactly would that look like? I would never initiate that kind of process."

"Well, the resignation would be your choice, and I would commend you for ministry opportunities elsewhere. I've said for a long time that if, for whatever reason, my presence here began to have a negative effect on the college, I would remove myself from this position because I want what's best for Wheaton College. I know you want what's best for the college."

"I guess we disagree on what's best, Dr. Ryken." I was frustrated to choke up in a professional conversation. "I'm primarily concerned about vulnerable students on campus and the message this would send to them. I still don't understand why you all hired me if you didn't want a gay person on staff."

"Like I've said before, if we had been aware of your public persona prior to hiring you, I'm not sure we would be in this position."

I stared at the carpet and breathed, trying to compose myself.

After a brief silence, he said, "Well, we're not there yet. I just wanted to put this on your radar as a possibility for the future."

o　o　o

That Sunday, when the Oak Park community gathered for our family dinner in Larycia's home, I was relieved to have a nurturing place to bring my sadness. After Larycia gave thanks for the food and refilled our wineglasses, I came out with my recent news: "Phil asked me to resign this week."

Christine audibly gasped and clasped her hand to her heart.

"What did he say?" Larycia asked.

"He said that because of the toll my presence is taking on the college, he could foresee a situation in which I would choose to resign, and he would commend me for ministry opportunities elsewhere."

"Well, you now have some very important information about how Wheaton is thinking about all of this," Christine said.

"Julie, how are you doing emotionally?" Larycia asked.

"I told him I would never initiate that kind of thing, but I don't know . . . I'm honestly just trying to make it through the days."

12

In late January, I was set to write a feature story for *Christianity Today* about gay celibacy and my role in helping shut down Exodus International. I wanted LGBTQ Christians to read it and think, "Wow, she's right: I have gifts to offer the church, not in spite of the fact that I'm queer, but because of it!" I wanted them to see how their orientation made them faithful friends, sensitive to the suffering of others, and fiercely committed to working for a just and equitable society. One's queerness affects their friendships, their relationship with God, the way they experience art and beauty. I wanted to encourage Christians to celebrate all the aspects of a person's gay orientation that are nonsexual because LGBTQ people reflect diversity in God's creation. I needed straight Christians to understand they could alleviate much of the shame gay Christians experience by celebrating the unique gifts we bring to our communities.

By the time I began writing the article, the tension between President Ryken and I was palpable. Based on our conversations, it was clear President Ryken saw homosexuality as a form of brokenness, not an expression of the beautiful diversity we see in the world. He seemed uncomfortable with the extent to which I liked being a lesbian. ("I wonder if 'lesbian' has more pejorative connotations for some Evangelicals," he said to me in an email. "You have used the term some in the blogosphere, and this has probably caused some consternation.")

I could've relieved the growing tensions between us if I framed my sexuality as a struggle, a sinful desire, a "thorn in the flesh" (like the one the apostle Paul famously described in the Bible as a "messenger from Satan," which he pleaded with God to remove, to no avail). The thorn in the flesh was a key biblical story used by conservative Evangelicals to describe a Christian's struggle with same-sex attraction. It was a framework that helped them tap into compassion for sexual minorities, and it was a step up from their previous understanding of gays as rebels who were out to get the Christians.

But I didn't want to add to the burdens gay Christians already carried by framing their natural sexual orientations in terms of "struggles" and "battles" and biblical images involving messengers from Satan. I simply could not write the kinds of words Wheaton's administration wanted me to write without contributing to the shame and anxiety queer folks experienced, adding more weight to their already unbearable burdens.

Before I sent the *Christianity Today* article to my editor, President Ryken asked me to send a draft to him, Stan Jones, and LaTonya Taylor. Stan responded hours later with a seven-paragraph email that was critical but also respectful of me and my essay. His tone was gentle, and he ended his email by saying I was a unique and beautiful person—his sister in Christ.

That email was from Stan Jones, the human being—which is distinct from Stan Jones, the provost of Wheaton College. Stan the human was humble, gentle, and a thoughtful conversation partner. Stan the provost was hired to enforce the will of the board of trustees and wealthy donors—people who were not interested in splitting hairs over whether sexual identities are socially constructed. These were people who needed gays to understand their place as broken, at best, and perverts, at worst. Stan was in a weird place too.

"You and I are walking in the same shoes," he said to me a few days later when we met to discuss our differences. "As much as I desire at times to speak my own mind, I can never step out of the role of representing Wheaton College. You are now in that same position."

I smiled and nodded, but I knew we were not in the same shoes. I did not represent Wheaton College. I had a growing awareness that I represented my people, which I was even more determined to do after sitting with countless queer students in their suffering. I represented a vulnerable and resilient community that the American people, in general, and Christians, in particular, had mocked, abused, vilified, and despised throughout our country's history. I represented the brave students at Wheaton College who woke up every morning in a community where they knew they were not wanted and showed up anyway.

When Stan said he represented Wheaton College, I understood he meant the people with money and power. That was not my Wheaton.

Then President Ryken weighed in on my essay: "I believe that as the article presently stands, it would generate very significant negative publicity for the College in ways that could affect Admissions and Advancement, and also make it hard for me to be as publicly supportive of you as I have been to date."

He went on to say, "A major issue, from my perspective, is that the piece gives the impression that homosexual desire is a created good rather than a form of brokenness—a desire for something that is not pleasing to God."

Stan jumped in with a heavy editing hand. And again, I did my best to synthesize Stan's suggested paragraphs, to incorporate President Ryken's commentary and LaTonya's revisions, and sent them a final draft the day before the essay was due.

The next morning, President Ryken responded: "As I survey the current draft, I remain very concerned that the impact on Wheaton College will be negative." He said he respected my right to publish it, but that it would be unwise for me to do so. He ended the email saying, "I see it as causing more trouble than the help it brings and would discourage you—even at this late date—from proceeding with publication."

A few hours later, I received a separate note from LaTonya: "Can you meet today?"

I didn't know what to make of LaTonya. She was one of the few Black women on staff at the college, and she let me know she was aware of the challenges I faced as a minority navigating Wheaton's political and social dynamics. She spoke freely with me in what felt like an unfiltered way. But her full-time job was to spin stories to protect Wheaton's image. She worked closely with President Ryken, and I always wondered if she was a direct line to me from him. At Wheaton, it was difficult to discern who was in your corner and who was a spy in the land.

LaTonya suggested we meet outside of the Billy Graham Center to go for a walk. It was the end of January in Chicago. The temperature rarely rose above thirty degrees. No one walks outside unless they absolutely must.

"What a day," she said, shaking her head as she approached me, her petite frame buried under layers to keep her warm.

We walked past the Blanchard building, where Dr. Ryken had an office, past the student center, beyond the tennis courts, gymnasium, and dorms, to a neighborhood that bordered the campus. LaTonya didn't say much for the first part of our walk. She let me tell her, once again, that I wasn't saying anything that went against the Community Covenant in this article.

"I highly doubt Ryken is personally editing articles from all the straight people at this college," I vented. "Is he emailing the dudes in the theology department at 4 a.m. to weigh in on their work? Is he asking straight staffers where they receive accountability for chastity?"

"Listen," she finally spoke up, once we were a safe distance from campus. "I don't want to show up in your memoir someday as the person who tried to silence some MLK for the gays, but I'm gonna be honest with you: if you go through with publishing this piece, I don't think you'll have a job here next year."

Panicked, I asked, "What do you mean? You think they would actually fire me, the first openly gay person who's ever worked at Wheaton? That's outright discrimination! That'll be an even bigger PR nightmare than my presence here has caused."

"I'm just being real with you," she said in a hushed tone, even though no one was in sight. "Only you can decide whether it's more important for you to have a public voice or to work here with students, but I'm telling you, you can't do both."

"Wow. Okay. This is some serious bullshit! Why the hell did they hire me, an openly gay writer and speaker, if they didn't want one on staff? Let them fire me—I'm a writer! Don't they know what happens when you discriminate against writers?"

We walked in silence down the empty suburban street while the news settled. After an extended silence, I asked, "Did Ryken tell you this directly? Is this like a threat to me from him or is this just a hunch based on your interactions with him?"

"All I'm saying is that if you want to work here next year, you need to kill this piece. And honestly, Julie, you may not even have until next year if you publish it. They might act swiftly to make a public display of the situation, saying something to the effect of 'We made a mistake in hiring her, but we took care of that mistake.'"

"Oh my God, LaTonya! They would fire me in the middle of the school year right after I publish an article that's tame enough to show up in *Christianity Today*? Jesus Christ!"

We walked in silence past trees with no leaves, making our way back to campus. I had considered the possibility that it might come to this, especially after my conversation with President Ryken a few weeks earlier. But this felt urgent. President Ryken and LaTonya were in close contact. They spoke often about my situation, and she was up to speed on his latest thoughts regarding my work. Maybe he told her to pass that on to me—a way of threatening me without getting his hands dirty. Or maybe she was looking out for me, warning me about the severity of this decision. Either way, the threat was looming.

"Well, I've got a few more hours before the deadline, so I'll think it over and let y'all know what I decide," I said once we got back to campus.

"I'm really sorry, Julie," she said as we parted ways. "I'll be on the lookout for a note from you this afternoon to see what you decide, and I'm around if you need to discuss anything between now and then."

A few hours later, I emailed the group: "Thanks for shooting me straight, Dr. Ryken. I'll be honest and say I feel very disappointed. I truly believe God has called me to Wheaton College, though, and I'm willing to make whatever sacrifices I might need to make in order to be faithful to the ministry He's called me to here at Wheaton. After prayerfully considering your advice, I decided not to publish this piece."

When I packed my things and went home for the day, my chest didn't feel tight. My anxiety was replaced by a deep sense of sorrow. The pit in my stomach felt bottomless. I didn't want to eat, or drink, or work out. I wanted to go to sleep and never wake up.

13

The Monday after I killed the *Christianity Today* piece, I locked myself in a bathroom stall in Wheaton's student center to scroll through the notifications on my phone. I needed to figure out why my phone had buzzed multiple times a minute over the last hour. Then I saw one of several texts from Gabe Lyons: "This is insane! Your talk is going viral." He finally got around to sharing the video from the talk I gave at Q Women a few months earlier in a rather controversial tweet that read, "Dear Christians: Hear a Christian lesbian tell us why affirming gay sex is not the only way to love gay people."

I put the lid down on the toilet, sat on top of it fully clothed, and buried my face in my hands. I was uncomfortable with that talk the moment I gave it because of the thirty seconds I spent defending traditional sexual ethics. Even though I was personally single and celibate, it felt problematic. I had comforted myself with the reminder that it was just one talk to a few hundred women.

"It was a learning experience," I said to Ezer the week after I gave the talk. Now it was spreading on the internet faster than germs move through a young family. On the heels of the drama surrounding my article for *Christianity Today*, I didn't have the will to live another day at the center of the Evangelical debate about queer people.

That's when it hit me—"I can leave." I had felt trapped, as if I lacked agency in Evangelical communities. For years, I had believed God's love for people was not contingent on where they landed on the question of same-sex relationships. The Holy Spirit was clearly moving in communities that fully affirmed queer people. I sensed God's delight in my friends who were in same-sex relationships. It wasn't God that I was afraid of—we were good. Why did I continue to capitulate to a system that used me, silenced me, and, at best, tolerated me?

Because I loved them.

These communities were not monolithic. Sure, there was Gabe Lyons and President Ryken, but there was also Larycia Hawkins and all the courageous students who loved the community enough to try to change it. Evangelicalism contained family members who worried when I was around their kids, but it also included the middle-aged mom at Wheaton who said, "You know, I asked myself, 'Would I want Julie to mentor my teenage daughter?' Yes, I think Julie would be an amazing mentor for my daughter!"

Since evangelicalism wasn't any one of those groups of people, I didn't want to let the fundamentalists have the last word. Somehow, I found myself in a position of relative influence in conservative Christian circles—something very few queer folks had. And I was making a difference. Parents of gay kids were moved to embrace their children after someone they trusted gave them permission. Folks lined up to meet me after I spoke, saying it all made sense to them for the first time: Of course people didn't choose to be gay! They didn't choose to be attracted to the opposite sex! Gay people were God's children, and they needed to be loved and fought for, not pushed away.

Then there were the actual queer people in those communities. Many of them felt seen for the first time when they met me or heard me speak. Suddenly, they felt less alone. They were able to imagine the possibility of a future full of love and connection.

How could I walk away from the earnest people who longed for the inclusive vision my friends and I were casting? How could I give up the opportunity to make life more bearable for my queer family? Besides, I reasoned with myself, beliefs are weird. You don't entirely choose them. It wasn't dishonest to remain in those communities as long as I didn't date women.

As long as I could thread that needle, I was going to stick around.

A few weeks later, Wheaton's campus was buzzing with conversation about an incident that occurred in the Town Hall Chapel earlier that Monday morning. The annual town hall gave students the opportunity to ask Wheaton's president anything they wanted. A straight student asked President Ryken why the Statement of Faith and Community Covenant, which lacked any language about sacraments that were central to Jesus's teaching (like baptism and Communion), formally condemned and denied equality to LGBTQ Christians on spurious theological grounds.

After President Ryken answered his question, the student turned to walk back to his seat, and that's when it happened: another student threw an apple at the guy who asked the question. Later that afternoon, the apple thrower posted a letter on the forum wall, a community bulletin board where students are free to express themselves. "Dear Enemy," the letter began. "You would be mistaken to think that I threw the apple out of hatred . . . No, I threw it purposefully as a warning against insulting the Spirit of grace. Because Truth itself was maligned. For the destruction of those who 'have the form of godliness but deny its power' was written about long ago." The student ended the letter saying, "Not ashamed of truth," and then signed his full name.

Queer students felt attacked. "A student was assaulted for speaking up for queer people in chapel!" Christopher cried out to me in the hallway outside of the school cafeteria. "The college needs to take action immediately. This is not a safe environment for LGBTQ students."

I told Christopher I would connect with Paul Chelsen, the vice president of student life, to find out how the administration planned to respond.

Christopher wasn't going to wait for the administration to act. In his fourth year at Wheaton, he had been around long enough to know how these things played out: Someone in Wheaton's administration may or may not release a vague statement saying they were sad to hear about the incident, all students deserve to feel safe and supported, and the Community Covenant forbids violence of any kind. They likely wouldn't name LGBTQ students specifically, and they certainly wouldn't get into the structural issues at play, like how the community's beliefs created the conditions for the violent outburst.

That afternoon, Christopher reached out to a reporter at *Time* magazine to inform them of the incident. Once that reporter reached out to LaTonya Taylor, the administration moved swiftly. Paul Chelsen called an emergency meeting with leaders in student development to discuss our plan of action.

President Ryken worked with LaTonya on the communications strategy. I met with queer students nonstop to give them space to process their feelings and to reaffirm their value.

Christopher also wrote a post on his personal blog, where he discussed broader, systemic issues at play in the events surrounding the incident in chapel: "The response of others following the incident disturbs me more than the action itself. I saw peers exert more effort into rationalizing the offense rather than demonstrating support to the LGBTQ community whose experiences were disrespected." He mentioned three responses he heard and concluded, "Each of these answers has one thing in common: they take responsibility off of the offending individual in an attempt to absolve this student of displaying any prejudice against a minority group."

Christopher's read of the situation was spot-on: both staff and students were inclined to see the homophobic incident in isolation. And while Christopher didn't know it, a group of student leaders quietly advocated for the apple thrower behind the scenes, explaining to President Ryken that the apple thrower was a social outcast and he didn't understand the stakes of his behavior. They pleaded with campus officials not to remove him from campus—didn't he deserve grace?

It seems like a reasonable response: we Christians believe in mercy. But the responses were also an example of the way many Evangelicals quickly call for grace for certain kinds of people: pastors who abuse their power in their relationships with women, white men who unleash gunfire where immigrants are gathered, Christians who use their faith as a weapon against queer people. Why do we call for compassion for some people and not others?

Christopher had been around long enough to know the one thing that moved the college to action: public awareness. By Wednesday afternoon, *Time* published a story about the events on campus that week.

"President Ryken did not see the incident and did not fully understand what happened until after chapel ended," Wheaton College told *Time* in a statement. "He asked our community to pray for leaders from Student Development and the Chaplain's Office who hold students accountable and work with them for repentance, healing, and reconciliation."

The article ends with a quote from Christopher: "It has been confirmed to me that as of this afternoon, the offending student will no longer be on campus, and if he is on campus, LGBTQ students that feel threatened will be immediately notified. I'm incredibly impressed at how the administration is responding—I'm very pleased to know they are taking this seriously."

If Christopher hadn't drummed up media attention, I don't know how the administration would have handled the apple incident. But I do know the situation was another example of Wheaton leadership believing queer students were cunning when what I saw was a group effectively advocating for their community. Christopher had tried to be conciliatory. For years, he gave Wheaton administrators the benefit of the doubt, meeting with them privately and trusting they would take action to make the campus safer for LGBTQ students.

After too many empty promises, Christopher realized he needed a new strategy. He wasn't trying to stick it to the college when he called public attention to injustices on campus; he'd simply given up on the idea of partnering with Wheaton leadership for change from within.

He didn't resent them for it. In fact, he believed many of them actually wanted to show more support for queer students, but their hands were tied because they had to consider donors, alumni, and trustees. As a student, his priority wasn't donors or trustees—it was vulnerable queer people.

The eruptions in the battle between LGBTQ students and administrators were clarifying for me. My theological beliefs were based on the authority of Evangelical leaders. Of course, Evangelicals say the Bible is their authority, but it's interpreted in thousands of different ways. When people say the Bible is their ultimate authority, each person has a different understanding of what the text means, which is largely shaped by the theologians and pastors they trust. I wasn't aware that I was reading the Bible with an interpretive lens because Evangelicals claimed to have absolute, objective truth. They didn't acknowledge their positionality, how their context shaped their understanding of the text, or how they read into the Bible just as much as they read from the Bible.

In Protestant communities, the issue of authority ultimately falls back on the individual because we choose to believe the teachings of one theologian over another, one pastor over another. I inherently trusted conservative Evangelical leaders because I was raised in a context where they were given total power. We followed their teaching or risked being kicked out.

When I arrived at Wheaton, I trusted that the people in power had the most insight into how LGBTQ students should live. I believed their assessments of queer students and figured they were right about people like Christopher—that he was just angry and hungry for attention. With each event on campus, however, I saw more clearly how the administration made decisions that benefited them, and it came at the expense of the most vulnerable. When students protested, it was because they were left with no other option. When they organized underground, it was because they weren't allowed to exist as their full selves out in the open.

Even under all that pressure and scrutiny, students still managed to organize with grace. By late spring, I wondered if LGBTQ Christians might have a better sense of what it meant for them to be faithful than the straight people in power.

14

At the end of April, I flew to Boston to speak at Q's National Conference. For the first time, a mainstream Evangelical conference was hosting a conversation between two gay Christians: I would share about my experience as a celibate queer Christian, and Matthew Vines, a gay Christian writer and activist, would lay out the biblical case for supporting same-sex relationships. Following that discussion, we would be joined by David Gushee, a leading Evangelical ethicist, professor, and minister, who had recently moved to support same-sex relationships, and Dan Kimball, a quirky pastor of a vibrant Evangelical church in California that was cutting edge in vibe, but theologically conservative.

I wasn't surprised when Gabe scheduled a call with just me and Dan about a month before the conference. Typically, the whole panel would be on a call like that so we could run through the flow of the event and discuss any questions, but the two LGBTQ-affirming speakers were noticeably absent from that call.

"Well, thank you both so much for making time to connect," Gabe started. "I think you two are going to be powerful witnesses and that people will really feel the contrast between the two of you on the one hand and Matthew and David on the other. I would love to brainstorm some questions here with you and run through my hope for the discussion."

He emphasized, once again, the need for me to make a strong call for Christians to hold fast to traditional teaching on sex and marriage. And once again, I told him that wasn't my main focus. As the conversation came to a close, Gabe invited us to a VIP party on the first night of the conference. Separately, Gabe also asked me to fly in a day early to attend an exclusive meeting with a handful of other leaders in his network called Axiom, and he asked if I would block off the day after the conference for another roundtable discussion about LGBTQ rights and religious liberty.

From what I could tell, Axiom was intended to be a sort of Evangelical elite—an invite-only club consisting of mostly white, male, business executives, thought leaders, lawyers, writers, activists, and pastors. The vibe of the group was similar to the roundtable I attended in San Francisco the summer before I went to Wheaton. There were monthly newsletters, occasional conference calls, regional gatherings, and an annual convening at a posh hotel on a beach, where a few dozen people flew in to network with one another and hear casual panel discussions from fellow members. There was an annual fee to be a member, but I gave brief talks at the meetings, and they never asked me to pay. They also didn't pay me for those talks.

On the morning of my dialogue with Matthew, I dressed in a purple and white checkered button-up with a navy-blue cardigan draped over it (my clothes were tight because I had gained weight from stress eating and drinking my way through the previous nine months at Wheaton). I rehearsed my lines once more in front of the mirror. Q stuck to a tight timeline: Matthew and I each had a total of nine minutes to answer three questions Gabe posed, which is a short amount of time to calm the audience's anxiety about my gayness, convince them I'm a real Christian, convict them of their complicity in our nation's violence against queer people, and walk the line of celebrating queer Christians while technically not affirming same-sex relationships.

The conference took place in Converse Hall in the Tremont Temple in Boston. The setting felt like a traditional theater, with dark wooden chairs, burgundy carpet, and gold rails propping up the two balconies that lined the three walls facing the stage. My stomach clenched from nerves as I slipped into the back row in the balcony for the morning sessions. I was out of my league.

The speeches that morning were powerful and moving. Each session centered on one theme, like racial justice or hospitality or the debate around death with dignity.

We heard from Native American leader Mark Charles, who talked about colonialism and the ongoing oppression of Indigenous people in the United States. (My education as a homeschooler in Texas failed to mention that the United States was not, in fact, discovered—it was stolen by violent force and then developed through slavery, concentration camps, and ethnic cleansing.) I wasn't aware of what the prominent speaker and writer Lisa Sharon Harper refers to as the "narrative gap" in our country's discourse, which consists of the contradicting stories passed down in different communities about our nation's history and current public life. While I was uncomfortable with the way Gabe stacked the deck in the dialogue about LGBTQ people, I understood Q also provided a platform for activists and leaders to educate Evangelicals about injustices that we might not be exposed to otherwise.

During the lunch break that afternoon, I tried to calm my nerves. The stakes were high: a prominent Evangelical conference had never featured queer speakers who discussed LGBTQ equality not simply in society but in the church. Even if Gabe seemed to quietly control the conversation behind the scenes, the presence of Matthew and me onstage together legitimized the debate. Our presence confirmed that gay Christians do exist, that we have a vital message, and that there are not clear answers to the questions we raise.

That afternoon, Matthew presented the biblical argument for same-sex marriage, and I said that I was committed to lifelong celibacy. But we both focused on the church's history of violence against the LGBTQ community. I told the audience of more than a thousand Evangelical leaders that they could not require gay people to commit to lifelong celibacy if they weren't prepared to help us bear the burden of loneliness that came with that demand. To make the point, I quoted Jesus's rebuke of the Pharisees in the Gospel of Luke: "And you experts in the law, woe to you, because you load people down with burdens they can hardly carry, and you yourselves will not lift one finger to help them" (Luke 11:46).

"We can live without sex," I said to the crowd, "but we can't live without intimacy." I said our society and our churches have told a single story of love and belonging that revolves around marriage and romance. We were going to have to imagine new ways of being together, where single people are integrated into the everyday lives of the families around them. It wasn't going to be enough for churches to have Tuesday night Bible studies and Sunday morning services; they needed to change the rhythms of their lives to create places of belonging for single folks. We wanted to join them on vacations and have meals in each other's homes when kids were whiny and kitchens were messy. We weren't interested in showing up to two-hour events and telling people about the lives we had lived since we were last together; we wanted to share our lives with them.

We crushed it. I struck the perfect balance, challenging conservatives without totally alienating them. While it's possible that my argument gave Evangelicals a way to support LGBTQ people without fully affirming same-sex relationships, it was a win for Matthew and for me to move the audience to see the humanity of queer people. They could imagine a church with leaders like us, people who expanded their imagination for the kinds of communities we could become.

Even a few years earlier, I couldn't anticipate a room of a thousand Evangelical leaders responding with such warmth and enthusiasm to a message that celebrated LGBTQ Christians. I would've given anything for Ricky and my mom to respond to me that way. When I was helping end Exodus, ex-gay leaders called me a heretic for sharing milder versions of the same message.

After the session, I couldn't walk three feet without someone stopping me to thank me or tell me about their gay family member. The founder and executive director of a conservative nonprofit that sought to advance free speech and religious freedom put her nose an inch from mine as she whispered her story about a sexual relationship she had with another woman years ago. She said she firmly believed I was uniquely called by God, set apart "for such a time as this" (Esther 4:14), a reference to Queen Esther in the Bible, who used her power and beauty to save her people.

Maybe it's because I'm a woman or because I talk genuinely about sexuality, but people I've never met often feel an intimate connection with me. After the talk, people felt permission to share things that began with "I've never told anyone this before, but . . ." Whatever their situation, I tried to be present with them, to look them in the eye and acknowledge the healing power of truly seeing people.

Then after the long set of stories, I made a beeline for the bathroom, where I locked myself inside a stall and exhaled.

This talk felt different than the Q Women one had. I had used my credibility with conservatives not to reaffirm their beliefs but to challenge them. All my years of turmoil felt worth it if I could move Evangelical leaders to see the queer people in their community as humans with value and dignity, resilient people with gifts to offer their churches.

Gabe asked me to stay a day after Q ended for another round-table discussion on religious freedom and LGBTQ rights. There were around ten of us this time: two prominent attorneys who specialized in religious freedom; the legal counsel for a large network of Evangelical colleges; the president of an Evangelical college who had recently come under fire for their treatment of LGBTQ students; a professor and a faith organizer, both of whom specialized in pluralism in the public square; the managing editor of a right-wing media outlet; a provocative, conservative blogger; a gay political writer who was known for being a contrarian; and me.

It was nice having another queer person in the room this time, particularly one who took up a lot of space. When the right-wing editor claimed Christians were more oppressed than

LGBTQ people in the United States, David lost it: "Oh, give me a break. We have no legal protection from discrimination in housing or health care. We can be fired simply because someone thinks we're gross. And this is after decades of Christians sitting on the sidelines watching thousands of people die in the AIDS crisis."

"Okay, everyone," Gabe piped up from the head of the table, cutting into David's diatribe. "Let's refocus this conversation on some of the current issues we're facing at Christian colleges."

Gabe seemed uncomfortable with the way David created sympathy for queer people.

"Christian colleges are ground zero for this debate right now, so I want to give Michael the opportunity to share an update on things at Gordon College." Gordon became a center for controversy in 2014, after Christian leaders sent a letter to President Obama requesting that religious employers be allowed to refuse to hire LGBTQ people and still receive federal funding. I later learned the letter was initiated by Gabe and that the president of Gordon College was among the signatories. When the letter became public, the regional backlash to Gordon from surrounding towns in Massachusetts was swift. The mayor of Salem canceled a contract with the college that previously allowed it to use its Old Town Hall facility. A local school ended its partnership with Gordon, refusing to accept student teachers from the college. Finally, Gordon's accreditor gave them one year to ensure that they did not have discriminatory policies, potentially threatening their accreditation. Media lambasted the college, and queer students, alumni, and allied professors were outraged. Gordon's policy that "forbids homosexual practice" drew nationwide attention as the gap between conservatives and progressives widened.

Conservatives in higher education were paranoid that Christian colleges might be forced to choose between their religious values and federal funding or accreditation, despite the recent Supreme Court ruling that Hobby Lobby did not have to provide birth control to female employees if it violated their religious convictions—a clear win for religious freedom advocates. And even though one week later, the Supreme Court said Wheaton College wouldn't even have to fill out a form that would make insurance companies responsible for covering the cost of birth control to female employees—an even more forceful decision in favor of religious liberty—Evangelicals believed the government was out to get them.

We got the update on Gordon: The last year had been tumultuous. The Gordon community had been embroiled in conflict ever since the letter to President Obama was made public. Students routinely protested Gordon's policies outside of chapel. The college faced backlash in their community, with a number of long-term local partners ending their relationship with them because of their discriminatory policies. Nevertheless, a few weeks earlier, their trustees unanimously voted not to change their policy.

The meeting wore on, and I grew weary within a group focused on lamenting what happened to Michael and Gordon College as if they were the primary targets for persecution in the United States. With trans women disproportionately murdered with impunity, Gordon College receiving bad press for exclusionary policies was not at the top of my list of concerns.

Several hours into the conversation, I blurted out, "I'm gonna be honest. I've defended you guys. I've said conservative Christians aren't truly homophobic—that you have these sincerely held beliefs, but you really do love gay people. I don't know, though. Now that I've seen how Evangelicals treat *celibate* gay people, I'm not so sure."

Horrified at the thought of breaking down in that meeting, I tried to fight off tears. I continued: "My friends and I face discrimination in churches and Christian organizations simply because of our unchosen orientation, even when we've made incredible sacrifices to try to live in a way that aligns with our understanding of Scripture. We're seen as traitors to the gays, and then we're outcasts among Christians."

No one knew how to respond, as my comments were clearly disconnected from the overall conversation. A few people waited for me to look up so they could hold eye contact and nod sympathetically. Then the conversation moved on to other items on the agenda.

After the meeting, David walked straight over to me and wrapped me up in a hug. He rested his chin on top of my head with a long exhale, and I let myself breathe into his chest as people shuffled around us. After holding me like that for several breaths, he stepped back, looked into my eyes with a knowing gaze, squeezed my hand, and said, "Hang in there, honey."

Gabe grabbed me before I left and thanked me for being so vulnerable in the meeting.

"I didn't realize things had gotten so bad at Wheaton. Let me know how I can support you as you're going through this. And whatever you do, don't quit. That would really set the movement back. Your costly obedience is making an enormous impact well beyond Wheaton."

"Thanks for the encouragement," I said, gathering my luggage to head to the airport.

When I got to the airport, I texted a friend: "Steve, the meeting today was brutal, and I don't know if I will survive evangelicalism." Then I boarded my flight and wept the whole way home. I was beginning to understand the political context in which all of this was happening: The Supreme Court was expected to rule on same-sex marriage within the next few months. Evangelicals knew marriage equality was likely to be the law of the land. They were looking for a new political strategy to avoid having to intermingle with LGBTQ people, which they believed would make them complicit in a sinful lifestyle. Their response was to create a political fight around religious freedom. Christian colleges were seen as the next battleground, since they could potentially lose federal funding and accreditation. The Supreme Court had ruled against Bob Jones University in 1983, when they attempted to use the First Amendment as a tool to allow them to reject interracial couples based on their religious convictions. Conservatives knew there was precedent for the IRS to revoke the tax-exempt status of a Christian institution if they discriminated against a class of people. So Evangelicals had to somehow demonstrate that they did not discriminate against LGBTQ people.

That's where I came in.

I was seen as one of a handful of unicorn gays who would parrot conservative views and shield them from accusations of homophobia. When Gabe introduced me to his circles and Wheaton hired me, I naively believed their hearts were

softening toward the queer community and that they wanted
to make room for us.

After nine months of roundtable discussions with Christian leaders, consultations with board members at Christian
organizations, and meetings with administrators at Evangelical
colleges, I was convinced their acceptance of people like me
was a political strategy. Not only did gay people with conservative theology guard them against accusations of discrimination, but we also served as convenient mouthpieces. By
inviting us into leadership roles, our presence allowed them to
ignore the claims of the greater LGBTQ community that said
Evangelical theology and institutional policies were harmful to
queer people.

How could I have been so foolish to think they actually wanted us?
I wondered to myself on the plane ride home. *I've been a pawn
in their battle against my own people.*

15

I survived the rest of the spring semester. Somehow, I got myself out of bed each morning, brushed my teeth, and squeezed into clothes that fit comfortably earlier in the school year. I bundled up under layers because Chicago still has snowstorms in May and then trekked the half mile to the train station in downtown Oak Park to endure another day at Wheaton College.

After the *Christianity Today* debacle, I resolved to lie low for the rest of the school year. In honest moments with my Oak Park family, I shared that I was having panic attacks that sometimes spiraled into emotional outbursts of intense rage and grief that scared me.

At the college, I endured meetings on the Sexuality Task Force, where administrators catastrophized about the state of religious freedom in America. I fulfilled my weekly duties, like praying with speakers before chapel services on Monday, Wednesday, and Friday mornings and holding space for queer students at Refuge on Tuesday nights. I tried to set aside my personal anxieties, listening with attention and compassion as students sought comfort in my office. Some were coming up on graduation and didn't know what they would do then. Others were quietly suffering in the aftermath of sexual violence, mental health crises, and loss of faith. I wasn't the only one moving through the days with a deep sense of sorrow.

Toward the end of the semester, Stan Jones invited me to his house to have dinner with him and his wife, Brenna. Over homemade chili, we shared stories about Texas and Wheaton, their volunteer work in their church, and the joys of friendship with their adult children. I was genuinely touched by the tenderness between them, nurtured throughout forty years of marriage. Stan said he understood this had been a difficult year for me and that he wished conversations about sexuality were less contentious. As he spoke, his hands trembled from the slow march of Parkinson's disease through his body. He said he often found himself wishing he could share personal opinions that he simply could not express in light of his public role as provost of Wheaton. Stan was a therapist at heart, a compassionate listener, a humble man with high emotional intelligence. Sitting across from him and Brenna at their kitchen table, I felt loved and valued. I knew that even if I landed in a different place theologically, Stan would still consider me his sister in the faith. I wasn't angry at Stan. I was angry at the forces beyond him that demanded he lead with religious dogma instead of his kind heart. It wasn't that evangelicalism consisted of bad people—it was that a broken system made good people behave in ways that caused great suffering for people who were different from them.

Somehow, the students and I made it to the end of the school year. After cheering for graduates at the commencement ceremony, I coasted through the last few weeks before my summer break began. I showed up late and left early. I walked to the park in the middle of the day to read books in the grass. I had been in survival mode for so long, I needed solitude to get back in touch with myself and develop a strategy for the road ahead.

My summer break started with a road trip from Chicago to the Black Hills in South Dakota with my Oak Park fam. Christine cotaught a course about colonialism, where the class spent two weeks in conversation with Native American leaders. Larycia and I went along for the ride. We stayed on the Pine Ridge Reservation, mourned at Wounded Knee, and hiked in the Badlands. I will never forget an image one man shared with us when we gathered: he said that sometimes when he hunts and kills a deer, he lies down beside it and spoons it as it bleeds out, weeping and thanking the deer for giving its life so that he and his family could eat. That kind of humility and gentleness came through in all of our interactions. Eager to acknowledge "Creator," those we met disproved everything I was taught about Native Americans.

The more I learned about white Christianity's role in the historical violence against marginalized groups of people, from the slaughter of Native Americans to the weaponization of the Bible to justify slavery, the more I questioned dominant views about LGBTQ people. I learned the Southern Baptist Convention was created as a direct response to the northern Baptist resistance to slavery. I read about how the roots of the Christian homeschooling movement can be traced back to the days when Black children began attending white schools. In the Evangelical community, leaders covered up our history of violence or acknowledged our ancestors were imperfect, but they never really repented.

That history of racism showed up in different ways. When I was a kid, faith leaders told me that interracial couples were "unequally yoked," a blatant misinterpretation of the apostle Paul's words from his letter to the church in Corinth. The only thing I remember being taught about Martin Luther King Jr.

was that he was rumored to be a womanizer. I never heard about his revolutionary work for civil rights or his galvanizing sermons. It was in step with the kinds of things leaders in my community said about Black preachers more broadly—that they were womanizers or closeted queers, that their teaching was heretical. No white adults in my tradition said that if we wanted to find God, then we needed to look to the Black church, where worship, service, and indomitable hope are a way of life.

Things were shifting inside of me. I didn't necessarily read a new theological argument and then change my mind; beliefs aren't formed that simply. I began to ask different questions: If the leaders in my community had been that blind to their own racism, if our leaders historically baptized violence against entire people groups and declared it holy in the name of God, then why would I trust their teaching about LGBTQ people? When I knew hundreds of queer Christians who were wholeheartedly devoted to following Jesus, why did I believe the straight pastors who said we were deviant, broken, and worthy of damnation if we fully embraced our identities?

The question for me was one of priority: if people in a dominant group interpreted Scripture in a way that was different from those in a disenfranchised community, and if the dominant group's beliefs led to suffering for that community, then I would listen more intently to the people who were historically silenced.

I began to see the biblical precedent for that approach to interpretation too. The Jesus of the Gospels prioritized the poor and the oppressed. He moved toward women in a society that said women didn't matter. He prioritized children, sick people, people without power. Over and over again, he embraced people who were seen as scandalous and disposable.

Evangelicals in my community often dismissed those stories about Jesus, focusing instead on other passages of Scripture plucked out of context. What if we were less defensive, though? What if instead of scouring the Scriptures for texts to back up our preconceived notions, we got curious about people who see in a different light?

What if we stopped to ask ourselves whether God might be moving in the people we previously thought were wrong, or broken, or heretical? What if we listened to them with a spirit of sincere humility, considering the real possibility that they might be right and we might be wrong—or maybe we're both a little right and wrong because the spiritual life is complex and multifaceted?

The last big shift I experienced was understanding the importance of including the body and emotions in the process of doing theology. Pastors in my community often dismissed everything but the mind, quoting Bible verses like "The heart is deceitful above all things" (Jeremiah 17:9) and focusing on the apostle Paul's exhortation to be transformed by the renewing of our minds (Romans 12:2). Especially around questions of sexual ethics, many Evangelical leaders would say LGBTQ-affirming interpretations of the Bible were motivated by fleshly desires, prioritizing experience over truth. The Evangelical message was clear: bodies were bad, feelings led you astray, emotions were suspect, and the heart was deceitful. In this system, only the mind, which is easily manipulated and controlled, could be trusted.

Those teachings have left many Christians feeling torn between their head and their heart. I knew in my heart and spirit that LGBTQ people were healthier when they were in communities that fully affirmed and celebrated them. Where many friends previously suppressed their natural desires for sexual connection until they couldn't take it and then binged on secretive, unsafe sex with strangers, queer people in affirming communities could bring their relationships into the light and receive the benefit of supportive structures. Others were drawn out of deep depression because they could finally use their God-given gifts of leadership in the church. Those in supportive communities were more capable of integrating parts of themselves that had once been fragmented by their efforts to suppress their sexuality. They were healthier, happier, and more connected with God, themselves, and their broader community.

By the end of my year at Wheaton, I had a clarity within myself: I had been happy for all my queer friends who fell in love and sensed God's delight in their relationships. While my head told my heart it wasn't supposed to feel that way, my intuition said the Holy Spirit employs emotions and experiences to guide us. Other Christian traditions include science and reason in the discernment process. When trying to figure out how God intends for us to live, they incorporate prayer, intuition, concern for mental health, historical context, and attention to the effects of our theology in the real world, for good or bad. If Jesus came so that we may have life, then why would God tell queer people to submit themselves to a system that leads to death—emotional death, relational death, spiritual death, and in some cases, physical death?

Of course, there's always the possibility that I could be wrong. It's what made me so fearful to come out about my evolving beliefs. The stakes were incredibly high: I would lose my job, be publicly shamed and alienated from loved ones, and if the fundamentalists were right, potentially spend eternity in hell.

But when I thought about the God I've known since I was a little girl, I remembered God is merciful. God saw the tears my queer friends and I cried for years in our beds at night. God heard our prayers and saw our desperate attempts to offer our bodies as sacrifices. God understands that it's really hard being human and that the task of interpreting Scripture is difficult. God knows we were created for relationships—that it's not good for humans to be alone.

If I was wrong to come to a place that fully affirmed LGBTQ people, then surely the God who sees and knows my heart would have mercy on me. I had done my due diligence. I had been willing to carry my own cross until death, if that's what it took. But I could not, in good conscience, burden vulnerable queer people when I saw their suffering and knew in my heart that it was the church, not God, making demands that caused their suffering.

Over the course of about a month, I started writing about my change of heart, just for myself. I wanted to make sense of my evolving views because you don't necessarily choose your beliefs. You suddenly realize that you have, for longer than you were willing to admit to yourself, been operating from a belief system that is different from your stated views. Maybe you hid those new beliefs from your conscious mind because it was too scary or sad to face the truth. That's what the division among the mind, body, and spirit does: it makes us lie to ourselves.

I wrote my way through my confusion, and I was the most honest I had ever been in my life. Not because I had intentionally lied before, but because I couldn't even tell the truth to myself.

I sat on the document for a few weeks, trying to figure out what to do now that I was aware of the discrepancy between my honest beliefs and the ones I was expected to assert in order to stay at Wheaton and maintain credibility as an Evangelical speaker.

Within a few weeks, the answer was clear: I needed to come out about my change of heart. I needed to share what I had written. I sent the 1,300-word essay to my Oak Park family and told them I planned to post it the following Monday on my blog.

Early on Monday morning, Christine showed up on my doorstep with a cup of coffee. We decided over the weekend that I would send my resignation letter to President Ryken minutes before publishing the post on my blog. I didn't have the fortitude to endure another round of meetings with Wheaton administrators. Why make them fire me when my outcome was simply to tell the truth, accept the consequences, and then begin rebuilding my life?

We assumed the post would be live around 9:30 that morning, 10:00 a.m. at the latest. I already had the draft ready to go on my blog—edits, keywords, tags, everything was set—so an hour or two was more than enough time.

By 10:00 a.m., I was curled up in a ball on my couch, weeping. For my entire life, I had believed a single story about the world: the Evangelical story. Every question of meaning and purpose—every future I tried to imagine for myself—was filtered through the lens of conservative Christianity. I had devoted my life to ministry and had no idea what I would do for work once I was disqualified from those circles. I spent half of my teens and all of my twenties trying to cleanse myself of the queerness that would cost me my family if it wasn't contained. How would I live with myself if I went against their wishes, against my mom's demands? At twenty-nine years old, I felt like I might cease to exist if my family rejected me once and for all.

Beneath the practical questions about my career and community were the existential ones that gave my life order and purpose. Who would I be if I was not a good Evangelical?

Every time I had dared to peek behind the curtains of the "good Evangelical" version of myself I had earnestly grown into, I faced shame and confusion. I grew up hearing, again and again, that at my core I was depraved, disgusting, broken, an enemy of God. I also heard that, without the Evangelical God, I was like filthy rags, like a rotten tree. To alleviate that shame, I did everything Evangelicals said would put me in good graces with God (and with them). How would I alleviate that shame once they disowned me? How would I become good?

By 11:00 a.m., I paced back and forth in my living room in my second change of clothes (I had already sweat through my first). We were ready to publish the post. We had multiple tabs open on my computer: a tab for my blog, a tab with my resignation letter, a tab with copy already written for my social media posts when I went to share the blog. We were organized, but I wasn't emotionally prepared.

How do you prepare yourself for the end of the only life you've ever known?

By noon, Larycia came over for backup support. She sat on one side of me, and Christine sat on the other. They listened to my anxieties and let me cry some more. At one point, they each placed a hand on my shoulder and prayed for me.

All day long, I looked for excuses not to publish the post. The emotions were similar to the ones that compelled me to move back into the Hope House after I tried to leave Living Hope and to double down on nonaffirming theology like I did after Pride in San Francisco. Part of me longed to run back to a story that promised stability—a story that would briefly make me feel like I was standing on solid ground again. Those narratives served me better than Prozac.

But I knew this time was different. I now understood it was anti-LGBTQ teaching that made me burn my body, made my friends turn to meth, and made Wheaton students fantasize about killing themselves. I could no longer allow my name or story to be used to serve a narrative that led to death.

Over the next three and a half hours, I cried harder, paced faster, placed my finger on the "return" key to hit "publish" on my post, and then tossed my computer aside and burst into tears again. I sweat through yet another set of clothes. And then, at 3:45 p.m., I took a deep breath, placed my finger on the "return" key, and pressed down. The post was live.

We moved to action. Christine hit "send" on my email to President Ryken. I shared my post on my social media platforms. Immediately, my phone started buzzing. Journalists shared it, saying, "Lesbian chaplain publicly endorses marriage equality." Progressives tweeted, "I've always loved you, Julie!" Conservatives texted to ask for clarity. My mom left me an emotional voice mail.

That evening, we took the train into the city to go to the American Indian Center of Chicago, where some friends held a meeting about saving sacred land in Arizona from miners. Christine and Larycia knew it wouldn't be good for me to sit at home alone, watching the internet shame me or celebrate me.

After the meeting, we took ourselves to the Green Mill, a historic jazz club in Chicago, one of our favorite spots in the city. I didn't check my email or social media. I silenced phone calls.

In the weeks that followed, millions of people would read and share my post. Speaking contracts would be dropped and old friends would shun me, confirming my fear that I would lose the community that raised me if I came to fully accept myself. But that night, my Oak Park sisters and I bought drinks and settled into a big red booth at the Green Mill to listen to jazz.

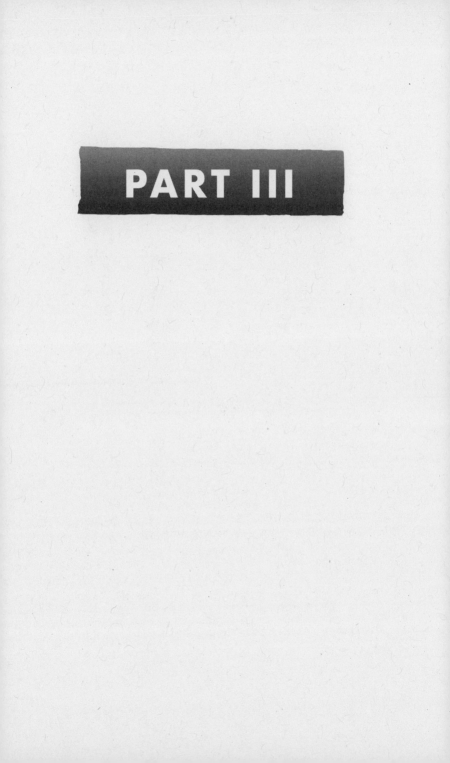

PART III

16

In September, when my friends finalized their syllabi for a new semester and back-to-school photos filled my social media feeds, I sat alone in my apartment in Oak Park. At some point, I would have to deal with questions of meaning and values, but first I needed a job. Not a career. Not a vocation. A job. A paycheck.

The problem was that I didn't know where I fit into the workforce outside of evangelicalism. While my peers hustled through internships and launched careers in their twenties, I worked in full-time ministry. And while I had transferrable skills, I didn't have a transferrable résumé.

Still reeling from my abrupt breakup with Wheaton, I lacked the fortitude to make big decisions about my future. So I turned to the industry that opens its arms wide to absolutely anyone looking for work. An industry that enthusiastically employs people who are undocumented, or fresh out of jail, or battling addictions, or dealing with the fallout of a theological shift that made them unemployable in their former line of work overnight. I went back to the food service industry.

On a chilly afternoon in Chicago, I took a train to the West Loop, home to some of Chicago's premier restaurants. Between the hours of 2:00 to 5:00 p.m., I bounced from high-end steak houses to sushi bars to diners until the general manager at Grange Hall Burger Bar offered me a job.

Jessica was a twenty-three-year-old, card-carrying lesbian, meaning she had an actual mullet in 2015. When I asked if they were hiring, she said, "We're fully staffed for servers and bartenders, but you could start as a busser and barback and wait around for something else to open up."

I didn't have time to wait for the ideal server job, so I told her to count me in and agreed to report to training the next day.

Grange Hall was a small establishment, a place without pretense, where people could show up at any hour of the day for a reliable burger and a craft beer or cocktail. There were around eighteen tables total, all in one room, with a bar that seated a few more. Of the roughly fifteen team members, three of us rotated shifts as the full-time support staff.

I had waited tables through college and was a manager at a pub in Dallas during graduate school, and while those jobs required long hours that stretched into late nights, they didn't give me a true appreciation for the work of a busser. At Grange Hall, my responsibilities included clearing tables when guests finished eating, running bins of dishes up and down the stairs, keeping ice and drink stations stocked, and taking all the restaurant's trash outside to the dumpsters behind our building, among other things.

My favorite shifts were Saturday brunches. I woke up early (by service industry standards) and put on dirty jeans and one of the four flannel shirts I set aside for work. Then I caught a train that dropped me off a half mile from the restaurant. Music welcomed me when I walked through the door of Grange Hall, and I would be greeted by the bartender and server who opened the restaurant. As I filled ice bins and helped servers roll silverware into napkins, we told stories and chatted about our lives.

In my role as an Evangelical speaker and chaplain, part of my job description required believing things about invisible realities (which may or may not have seemed true or life giving). It required me to strive to have a different sexual orientation—and to actively suppress the one I did have—every moment of every day. As an openly gay person who was invited into faith spaces, I felt pressure to be perfect. Every speech, every tweet, every prayer I offered in a group setting was under scrutiny. In the eyes of my Evangelical colleagues, I represented all queer Christians. I felt the responsibility to prove that we weren't depraved. My body was worn down from the grind of carrying unbearable burdens.

What a relief to report to my shifts at Grange Hall, where it didn't matter what I believed or who I was attracted to or what I had done the night before. All I had to do was stock service stations and take out the trash.

The juxtaposition between my former work and newfound freedom was vivid when I took out the trash one Saturday night. It was approaching midnight, and it was late enough in autumn for freezing rain and snow. The trash bag from the bar was particularly heavy that night. All of the waste adds up: the half-eaten burgers, melted ice cream, leftover fruit from the bar, unfinished beers. It piles up and warms up, sloshing around until there's a collection of trash juice at the bottom of a bag that weighs more than many of us can lift in the weight room. My job was to dispose of that trash in the dumpster behind our building. So I tied up the bag, pulled it out of the can, and slung it over my right shoulder to carry it through the hallway and outside the back door. Normally, I held the lid of the dumpster up with my left hand and used my right arm to toss the trash bag into the bin. After several failed attempts to get the bag up over the top of the dumpster, I had to accept that I could not fling this trash bag into the bin with one hand.

I pushed the lid over the back of the dumpster and grabbed the bag with one hand on top and one hand on the bottom. Squatting down in front of the dumpster with both hands on the bag, I engaged my core to activate as many muscles as possible and exploded upward, thrusting the bag up onto the ledge of the dumpster. And then the bag ripped. The trash juice—milk, beer, soda, ketchup, melted ice cream— burst from the bag onto me, drenching my clothes.

I let the bag drop to the ground and stumbled backward, soaked and defeated. *What are the circumstances of my life that led me to this moment?* I thought to myself.

Then it hit me: Sure, I was covered in trash juice, but I would never again face discrimination from my employer simply because of who I am. I wouldn't be told what to say when I was given a microphone or interrogated about where I received accountability for chastity. I wouldn't have to respond to a single person who asked me why I used the word *gay* to describe myself, who recommended I "find my identity in Christ" instead of my sexuality.

Even as I was covered in trash juice, I knew I had made the right call. I wasn't sorry. I wasn't wistful for the days when I was conditionally invited to walk the halls of power. To me, the trash juice dripping down my arms felt like freedom.

My time at Grange Hall reconfirmed my calling in many ways. When I became affirming, stepping over the line Evangelicals had drawn that determined who was in and who was out, I didn't know whether my faith would survive. Many of my friends left the church after they came out. They felt like they'd been duped. They had believed they were following God's call on their lives when they were actually caught up in a system with political and financial interests, whether those in their immediate communities knew it or not. Disillusioned and often depressed, they didn't see a path forward in the faith. In the weeks leading up to my public statement expressing support for same-sex marriage, I wondered if that might become my story as well.

I was surprised to find that on slow days, when I rolled silverware with servers to pass the time, several of them jumped at the opportunity to tell me about their history with the church. A bartender named Casey said that when he was a young college student, he felt called to be a youth pastor. He had been a leader in the youth group, and as a recent graduate, he was closely mentored by the youth minister at his church where he volunteered. He eventually told the pastor he was gay, and with that, he was removed from the volunteer team and pushed out of the church. Crushed and confused, he moved from his small town in Wisconsin to Chicago, where the men in the particular gay scene he got into were hungry for fresh faces. An older man took him under his wing, gave him a place to stay, and introduced him to meth. In a free fall after his ejection from evangelicalism, Casey found comfort in the drug scene, and he suffered emotional and physical abuse from the man he lived with for several years. One day he came home to find the man had packed up all of his things. He told Casey he was leaving, and on the way out, he said, "Oh, by the way, I'm positive. You may want to get tested."

Casey told me he lost his sense of purpose after he was kicked out of youth ministry. "I have good friends now and make good money and have health insurance, but I'm honestly still trying to put the pieces of my life back together."

All I could tell him was that his church had absolutely failed him. They lied to him about his worth and value. They did not speak for God when they said he wasn't worthy of love.

Our conversations didn't change Casey's life, but he did feel seen. Our encounter was an occasion for a small measure of healing.

Then there was Sam, the tall, baby-faced, tenderhearted bartender trying to make it as an actor. On slow nights, Sam and I snuck out to the back alley, where he shared his cigarettes and struggles with me. He longed to be reconciled with his Evangelical family, but they refused to meet the man he was engaged to marry. They said they "disapproved of his lifestyle." Even though they had been estranged for years, his voice still cracked when he spoke of his love for his family and his hope for reconciliation.

"Seriously, *how* am I just meeting you?!" Sam asked me in the alley one night. "I've always felt like no one in my Christian world believes that I actually love Jesus since I'm gay, and no one in my gay world could possibly understand my faith. You are the *first* person I've ever met who's super gay *and* a Christian, and I feel so seen!"

One of my favorite books in college was *The Scarlet Letter*, a historical novel about a Puritan community set in Massachusetts Bay in the seventeenth century. In the story, a woman named Hester Prynne has a brief affair with a minister, and she becomes pregnant with his child. The Puritans see this as a capital crime, so they publicly shame her, throw her in jail, and force her to wear a scarlet-colored *A* on her chest for the rest of her life. When she's released from jail, they banish her from their immediate community, so she buys a small cottage at the edge of town and makes a modest living as a seamstress.

At night, though, when the town went to sleep, members of the community begin to show up at her doorstep unannounced to confess their sins. They find comfort in her ability to sympathize with them in their sorrows. The novel's narrator says, "Her breast, with its badge of shame, was but the softer pillow for the head that needed one. She was self-ordained a Sister of Mercy; or, we may rather say, the world's heavy hand had so ordained her, when neither the world nor she looked forward to this result. The letter was the symbol of her calling."

I began to identify with that story as a busser and barback at Grange Hall, when I held space for people to process their pain, their unresolved questions, their longing for a redemption they couldn't quite articulate. The gatekeepers of evangelicalism said I was disqualified from formal service. They drew a line around their understanding of orthodoxy and purity and said I was on the other side of that line. But God was not confined to the boundaries they drew. I was still a chaplain; I just wasn't a chaplain who wore pressed shirts and dress shoes in the halls of power. Instead, I wore slip-free black sneakers and smelled like sweat and beer. On the sticky restaurant floors, through clouds of smoke in back alleys, God drew near to people through my lesbian body.

17

I burst through the revolving door at the Public Hotel, relieved to escape Chicago's windy snow. It was almost December of 2015, and I was five months into my new life as an extremely out, fully affirming lesbian. I hadn't planned on dating. My decision to become affirming was rooted in my support for *other* queer people, not myself. I was thirty years old, and I had been formed by two decades of teaching that said my body, my desires, my affections were disordered. I wanted to give myself time to live into a theology that celebrated my sexuality so that, if I ever did decide to date or marry, I could enter into that relationship from a place of integration, not disorientation.

A month before I walked into the Public Hotel, I was at brunch with my friend David, and during a break in the conversation to scroll through our phones, he suddenly squealed. His blue eyes lit up, and dimples formed in his light beard. "Oh my God, I have the biggest Instacrush on this super hot lesbian named Amanda Hite! Look at her!"

David flung his hand over his heart and thrust his phone in front of me.

"Wow, she *is* super hot," I said, pulling her account up on my phone. She had a sexy masculine energy, short black hair, and an androgynous style with a feminine twist. Her face was striking.

"Her style is on point!" David gushed. "Her hair, her tattoos, her jewelry, her whole vibe—it just *works*."

Then the next day, with no contact from me, I got a notification on my phone that read, "@amandahite followed you on Twitter."

I almost dropped my phone, horrified that I had accidentally liked one of her photos from two years ago. I hadn't followed her. I left no trace behind when I scrolled through her old posts. What prompted her to follow me when David and I had just casually stalked her the day before?

Embarrassed that I might have accidentally liked something from years ago, and curious about why she followed me, I did something I rarely do: I followed her back on Twitter and sent her a short message, saying, "So glad to be connected! Let me know when you're in Chicago—I'd love to grab coffee and share stories."

She responded within minutes and, uncharacteristically for both of us, we continued messaging throughout the day. The next morning, I woke up wondering how to proceed—should I continue the conversation? Also, why was I exchanging messages all day with someone I didn't know? And what was her perception of what was happening?

It was Halloween, so we sent each other photos of kids winning the internet with their cute costumes. We found an excuse to talk on the phone a few days later, and a week or two after that, she said she had a work trip in Chicago and wondered if she should come a little early or stay late so we could get dinner. We were going to meet in person.

I scanned the lobby of the Public Hotel, removing my coat and patting my clothes, trying to make myself look cute after the ninety-minute commute through heavy snow. Then I spotted her. She sat at a small table by a marble fireplace, chatting with a colleague. I was relieved that someone else was there to ease the tension, since we didn't yet know if we would hit it off in person. We knew there was mutual interest, but we hadn't discussed it. Both of us wanted to get a feel for what the other was like in person to avoid the awkward, "Oh, I was into you until I met you!"

Amanda leapt from her stool and wrapped me up in her arms. Her hug was firm and warm, and I was relieved to feel a magnetic pull between our bodies. One of my fears had been that I was going to be physically awkward around her. Having had zero romantic interactions in the last seven years, I was worried I would step on her foot when we went to hug or give her a one-two-three pat on the back when someone with more game might melt into her.

"It's so great to meet you in person!" Amanda said with her arm around my shoulder. "This is Eugene—he works with me, and we were just catching up for a bit before he heads out for the night."

I shook Eugene's hand and sat down on a stool next to Amanda, wishing I could remove my sweater without it ruining my outfit. My nerves had me sweating already, and we weren't even five minutes into the evening. Amanda was so gorgeous that I could hardly look at her. I didn't have the capacity to feel so attracted to someone and still form words, so I fired questions at Eugene for the first thirty minutes and focused intently on him. It gave my body time to get used to the fact that I was sitting next to an extremely attractive woman who had a warmth about her, a magnetism, an irresistible energy.

"I still know nothing about her as a person," I reminded myself. "We're just two human beings, with our share of flaws, wounds, and insecurities, and tonight is about getting to know the human who is Amanda Hite, not the fantasy I've built up in my imagination." My self-talk only calmed me a little.

We settled into comfortable conversation when we transitioned to the restaurant at the hotel. Over kale salads and french fries, we shared stories of growing up gay in conservative Evangelical families. Amanda's father was in the military, so they moved every couple of years throughout her childhood. That meant she moved in and out of different churches, which gave her insight into the arbitrary nature of the various moral codes of each community. One year they were allowed to celebrate Halloween, and the next year they were not. One year they could watch *The Smurfs*, and the next, it was forbidden. If the rules changed from church to church, then why would she trust their authority when it came to her sexuality? She left the faith behind when she turned eighteen and set out to feel her way to truth through reason and experience. But in the two decades she was away, she often felt drawn back to faith. Occasionally, she woke up early on Sunday mornings and drove to one of the large churches she saw from the road on her commute to work.

"It was honestly triggering for me—all the smoke machines and Christian karaoke."

I almost choked when she referred to Evangelical worship services as Christian karaoke.

"It wasn't until I moved to DC and attended a Pride service at the Washington National Cathedral that I finally felt at home in a church. After the marriage equality ruling, they had a celebration called 'Honoring the Road to Love and Justice,' and when I walked into the cathedral, people wore tie-dyed shirts and waved rainbow streamers. I cried the whole entire service. Gay Christians shared their testimonies, and trans ministers led us in prayer. I couldn't believe I hadn't known that was a thing! I had no idea there were churches that fully affirmed gay people and celebrated our love. Then I started going to services at the cathedral, and they were so *reasonable*. On my first Sunday there, the priest started his sermon by telling everyone to go vaccinate their kids. They made me feel like I didn't have to leave my brain at the door. After services, I walked down to little chapels on the lower level and spent time alone in silence. When I lost my grandfather and went through a deep depression, the cathedral was the only place where I felt truly at peace."

We marveled at the fact that we went in opposite directions at age eighteen (she moved away from the church of her childhood, while I doubled down and tried to become straight), but our disparate paths led us to the same place at that moment in time: lesbians with a love for Jesus and the Episcopal Church.

Amanda took me on a tour through her baggage during that dinner as well. She told me about her biggest mistakes and outlined some of the ways she needed to grow. I didn't expect that kind of vulnerability, but it made sense to me later: she was the founder and CEO of a digital marketing company that was on *Inc.*'s list of the top five hundred fastest-growing private companies in America that year. She was a busy woman. Dating someone can be all-consuming. She didn't want either of us to waste our time only to learn things months later that would have been deal-breakers up front.

The other issue she wanted to discuss was my theology. She had googled me. She first came across me when my post about becoming affirming was reposted in the *Washington Post*, and she was interested to know more. She watched my talk from the Q conference and said she was into it until the part when I said I "just wasn't persuaded by revisionist theology." She wanted to know why I called affirming theology "revisionist" and how I went from giving that talk—posted six short months ago—to advocating for same-sex marriage. It helped a little when I said the talk was posted six months after I gave it, but that was still only a year. She wanted to know if I unequivocally supported same-sex relationships or if I was still working out my theology. She didn't have the capacity to get involved with someone who was going to go back and forth about the morality of our relationship. She was done with that debate. If I was still in process, we could absolutely be friends, but she couldn't let herself fall for someone who wasn't settled on the goodness of queer relationships.

I told her my whole story: that I had supported same-sex love in my heart before I could acknowledge it in my mind, that I had been on the verge of becoming affirming for years and then my experience with Evangelicals in power pushed me over the edge, that my growing understanding of the way white Evangelicals used Scripture to enslave and oppress people of color shed light on my view of biblical authority, and that I dragged my feet on the path to becoming affirming because I was afraid of losing the people I loved most. I wouldn't have made a statement that alienated me from my community and cost me my job if I didn't wholeheartedly believe it.

She was convinced. She held my story with gentleness and compassion. I felt safe with Amanda. She tried to see the world through other people's eyes to understand how they arrived at their current viewpoint. She was clearly intelligent, so her grace for others didn't come from a place of naivete. As far as I could tell, it came from a pure heart.

After our long dinner, Amanda called a car for me so I wouldn't have to take the train back home in the snow. She wrapped me up in another full-hearted hug and gave me a kiss on the cheek before sending me on my way. My heart raced as I replayed our evening together in my mind. I couldn't resist the urge to text her on the ride home to tell her how much I enjoyed our night together. Before I finished writing my message, a note from her came through. The moment of truth! She said she was excited to see me again. I wanted to scream and squeeze my driver. I wanted to pop open a bottle of champagne and pour it all over my body. I liked—and respected and *wanted*—a woman who liked me back, and I had nothing to hide, no one to fear.

When I went home for Christmas one month later, I didn't tell my family I was seeing someone. My visit was brief, since food service workers get limited time off for the holidays, but forty-eight hours was long enough for me to acknowledge the truth I had been slow to accept: I didn't belong in my family.

I always imagined a family would break up the way lovers part ways, with an explosive conversation or series of conversations in which one or both people said they were done. I imagined a litany of offenses, a lot of tears, and a formal acknowledgment that the arrangement no longer worked. I pictured closure.

That wasn't how my last visit with my family went, though. Like every other Christmas before, we watched kids open presents, the oldest screaming about football jerseys while the youngest gazed with wonder at the wrapping paper. My brothers asked questions about the weather in Chicago and working in restaurants. What struck me was that no one asked about my personal life. They avoided discussions about my departure from Wheaton or my public ejection from evangelicalism. They didn't ask who I spent time with or what questions occupied my mind. They didn't want to know who was important to me or if I mattered to anyone else.

When I settled into my seat on the airplane that would take me away from Dallas for the last time, I finally asked myself the sad question, *What do you do when you love a family that can't or won't love you back?* They believed they loved me. But they had ingested years of religious teaching that said "love" looks like a refusal to acknowledge or accept the queer parts of their queer friends and family. Their religious leaders said that if they approved of my gayness (by which they meant me), they would be complicit in sin and, on judgment day, my blood would be on their hands.

I imagine my family thought it was kinder not to ask me about my life than to ask and hear answers that would require some sort of response. Maybe their apparent disinterest in my life was actually a tiny white flag of surrender, a way of saying they didn't want to disown me so, please, could I help them maintain ignorance, and with it, possible innocence. They were likely doing the best they could.

I began to wonder, though: Can you really love a person you refuse to know? For the first few decades of my life, I was willing to abandon myself to maintain a connection with them. After that visit home, I lost the will. I decided to bring my full queer self to my family from that day forward. Only then would I find out if they could love the real me.

o   o   o

Amanda and I were officially dating. The next time she came to Chicago, I knew we would kiss, and I hadn't kissed anyone in seven years.

I anxiously texted my friend Steve in the lead-up to her visit: "Steve, what if I don't know what to do with my tongue!!!" He reassured me that it would all come back to me: "It's like riding a bike!"

It was like riding a bike, and I was thrilled to find we had chemistry in every way. I started taking long trips to Washington, DC, in early 2016, staying a week or two at a time so Amanda and I could get a sense of how we were together in the monotony of everyday life. I still worked in restaurants, but I had also picked up contract work as a ghostwriter, so I had the flexibility to work remotely. Through the winter and into the spring, during my long visits to DC, Amanda continually impressed me with her integrity and generosity.

We took things slowly in the bedroom because I wanted to make sure I wasn't setting my ethics aside just because I was hot for Amanda. All of my formative years were spent in communities that said sex was bad, evil, and immoral unless you were in a monogamous, lifelong, heterosexual marriage. Even though, according to some surveys, more than 80 percent of single Evangelicals admit to having sex before marriage, the Christians in my community still set the bar at abstinence and accepted nothing less. I had come to see conservative teaching on sex as harmful in most cases: The culture of shame around sex increases instances of sexual assault and unsafe sex because people are more inclined to act on impulse rather than having thoughtful, caring conversations about intimacy.

I knew the sexual ethic I was handed wouldn't serve me, but I was also wary of creating a new ethic based on my impulses. I wanted to be thoughtful about it, to think theologically about sex in a way that was realistic, considerate, and wise. Through it all, Amanda was patient with me, careful to follow my cues rather than set the pace for us. We engaged in what we came to affectionately refer to as "not sex" while my mind, body, and spirit got comfortable with a sexual ethic that felt life giving.

My lease was up in Chicago in the summer of 2016, and there was no question about what that meant: I was moving to DC. In my first few weeks there, my friend Kirsten hosted a small gathering in her home to welcome me to the city. With that, we had a community. Kirsten's partner, Robert, was a kind-hearted man and a brilliant journalist. I also had a few other DC friends who happened to work in media. We were invited to book clubs and brunches, where we made new friends through those friends, and my network of people who supported my relationship with Amanda expanded.

Amanda and I became more involved in the LGBTQ community in DC, and we were delighted to develop a friendship with one extraordinary lesbian couple in particular: Kris Perry and Sandy Stier, the lead plaintiffs in the legal case that challenged Proposition 8 in California. Their case went all the way to the Supreme Court, where Prop 8 was ruled unconstitutional, paving the way for marriage equality a few years later.

History books will remember them as heroes in the movement for LGBTQ rights in the United States.

When Amanda first told me about Kris and Sandy's work, I didn't know anything about Prop 8—I just knew they were incredibly kind and hospitable. They embodied many of the character traits Jesus lauds in the Gospels. To know them is to adore them, which is why I was stunned to hear how conservative Evangelicals disparaged them during the fight for marriage equality. Through violent voice mails and slander in the media, Evangelicals told Kris and Sandy that God hated them and Christians were disgusted by them.

Exodus International was heavily involved in the fight for Prop 8. Even though at that point I was only loosely connected to Exodus, attending the national conference every summer with a group from Living Hope, I was horrified and ashamed when I learned that the community who I would've considered "my people" when Prop 8 was passed had vilified the women who were so dear to me and Amanda now.

The more I allowed myself to learn through experiences, the clearer it became that Evangelical leaders had willfully lied about the people I loved. They didn't simply express misguided views out of ignorance. They actively spun stories that denigrated beautiful queer people, drumming up fear in Evangelicals to mobilize them to support their preferred policies in every sphere of society. I did not want to believe that. But time and again, my interactions with warm, compassionate, kindhearted LGBTQ people disproved everything Evangelical leaders had said about them. It is not a coincidence that conservative Christian arguments continually benefit certain groups of people at the expense of others.

As I settled into life in DC, I couldn't believe how comfortable I began to feel in my body. A full 10 percent of adults living in the district are LGBTQ, making it one of the gayest cities in the country. I underestimated how much of an impact our context has on our mental health. Where in Dallas and at Wheaton I felt deeply insecure, always self-conscious about how I was perceived, in DC I could exhale. I didn't worry about how I walked or dressed. In a city with rainbow flags up year-round, where you see folks with beards in high heels and cute gays in tailored sweatpants, you quickly realize most people don't care if you're queer.

I hadn't known how much anxiety my body had absorbed in almost every social situation I had been in throughout my life. It was second nature for me to police my dress, posture, and mannerisms. Curbing my lesbian tendencies had been like blinking my eyes, a reflexive habit that I performed continually throughout my days with little awareness. Within months of moving to DC, I noticed my shoulders were less tense and my stomach relaxed. It was easier to breathe.

18

My growing awareness of the way conservative Christians had grossly misrepresented queer people coincided with Donald Trump's rise to power. As I grieved the loss of my Evangelical community, Trump swept the Republican primaries and secured his position as the GOP's candidate for president of the United States. I watched dumbfounded as leaders who denigrated me and my queer friends lined up behind Donald Trump, even after he was caught on tape bragging about sexually forcing himself onto women.

As I anxiously waited for Evangelical leaders to denounce Trump, one after another took to social media to defend him, saying that no one is perfect and we all deserve forgiveness.

I vented my frustration online: "I sure do wish Christian Trump supporters had been able to tap into all this grace and forgiveness when my LGBTQ friends and I came out," I tweeted. Obviously, I don't think I need grace or forgiveness for being gay. A sexual orientation—be it gay, straight, bi, or otherwise—is morally neutral. But the Evangelical community never extended kindness to the LGBTQ community the way they lavished it on Trump.

The most painful part of this, by far, was that close friends and family members who stopped speaking to me after I came out fell in love with Donald Trump. They didn't "hold their nose" and vote for him. They didn't vote for him and then go home and take a shower. They enthusiastically thanked God for a candidate who they believed would fight for them like no other president had. I took it personally.

I wondered if Evangelicals' objection to LGBTQ people, and maybe their doctrine more broadly, was never about theological beliefs but about power and cultural dominance. I watched ministers like Robert Jeffress, pastor of First Baptist Dallas, attempt to weave the two together, crafting theological arguments to support a worldview that functionally supported white Christian nationalism. And I couldn't help asking, How could loved ones who watched me spend more than a decade of my young life trying to live up to their standards accuse me of personal bias and not see the hypocrisy in their embrace of Trumpism?

On the heels of my eye-opening conversations with Evangelical leaders during my time at Wheaton, the 2016 election pummeled me. I couldn't believe I had given the entirety of my teens and twenties to a movement that was more concerned with power and self-protection than caring for the most vulnerable. I now understand what so many people of color and folks from all kinds of marginalized groups have been saying for so long: this has been a trend throughout white evangelicalism's history. The 2016 election was simply the first time my eyes were opened to it.

I started to wonder if I had actually been involved in a cult, especially at Living Hope. How could I have believed teaching that altogether denied medical research and the traumatic stories of ex-gay survivors? How was I so blind to the outright misogyny, the homophobia, the authoritarian nature of the whole enterprise?

As Evangelical leaders lost all moral authority for me, I became skeptical of everything else they taught me. It was difficult to read the Bible because they had twisted so many passages to support beliefs that clearly went against the teachings of Jesus. I could accept the possibility that humans misled me because of their personal biases. We are all products of our context, and if I had gone on to become a leader in ex-gay circles, I would've perpetuated the same toxic narratives. It's not hard to have grace for human flaws. What confused me was the way I had fused Evangelical leaders with God. I truly believed God spoke to me and told me things that I am now certain God never said to me. What I understood to be God's voice was Ricky's voice or my mother's voice, an echo of the human voices I valorized. How could I discern God's voice then? What was actually happening in prayer if it was only a product of my imagination? Had we simply made all of this up to create meaning?

My questions compounded, and my faith unraveled well into the years that followed. Evangelicalism had provided a structure for my entire life. It gave me answers to existential questions like Why are we here, Where did we come from, Where do we go when we die, and What's our purpose in the meantime? It also answered more immediate questions like What do I do with my mornings, my sexual impulses, my difficult colleagues? There was no question I came across, no problem I faced, to which evangelicalism did not dictate a clear and authoritative answer.

The problem wasn't simply that I needed to find new answers to these questions. My real anxiety was that the comfort I found in Evangelical clarity wasn't necessarily about the

answers—it was about how to find them. My religious system
had given me tools for interpreting the world. How do we
know what's true? The Bible says so! Who gives us a definitive
response when the Bible seems unclear? The men in charge!
What am I supposed to think about this new book that challenges some of our assumptions? Evangelical thought leaders
and publications will tell me.

With enormous existential questions and a lack of tools
to navigate them, I slipped into a free fall. Even if God had
audibly answered the questions I was asking, how would I
know that it was God and not the author of the last book
I had read or my own internalized fears from spending all of
my formative years in an authoritarian community? I could turn
to different denominations or faith traditions (which I did),
but they failed to provide the certainty (and with that, comfort)
that I longed for. I now understood what it was like to put all
of your trust in imperfect leaders and then later feel duped.

What I faced was a crisis of authority: I could look to a
liberal mainline church for answers, but I would be the one
choosing to place myself under that particular authority, and
I would always know it was *me* who made that choice. If I
choose which authority figures to follow, the burden falls back
on me to know what is best, right, and true. Part of me longed
to return to the days when decisions were made for me, when
truth was entirely knowable and uncomplicated.

This is what it looked like practically: I would wake up, make
myself some coffee, and think to myself, *What should I do with
this Tuesday?* To answer that question, I would think, *Well, I need
to know what I'm going to do with the rest of my life to figure out what to
do with this Tuesday! Should I apply for a job in communications? Should*

I apply to law school? Should I look into divinity schools and become a priest or a chaplain? No! I can't bear the thought of taking courses on eschatology! Besides, I've already felt the burn of having my finances tied to my faith and then experiencing a shift in that faith that disqualifies me from my previous line of work.

By the second cup of coffee, I had new anxieties: *How do I know I won't experience another shift that would disqualify me from a new iteration of religious employment?* Then I would pray about it, asking God to illuminate my path, and I would be overcome with panic within minutes of prayer. *I thought God was calling me to be an ex-gay leader when I was a kid and that's because I was in an actual cult—why would I trust that I could hear God's voice clearly now? I don't know if God is actually there or if humans made this up to create order and meaning. And if God isn't there, if life is random, then there is quite possibly no meaning, and it doesn't matter what I do with my life or what I do with my day.* Then I would scroll through Twitter.

I felt the weight of this crisis at the same time that I fell deeply in love with Amanda. For the first time in my life, I was at peace in my body. Not only was I at home in my body, but I was *seen* by someone else in an intimate way. Where previously love had been conditional—*if I'm good enough, then they'll love me*—I was now seen for who I actually was and loved in that place.

On evenings and weekends, when Amanda and I were on dates or eating takeout with friends, I sensed that I was waking up to myself. When I no longer had to suppress my sexual and romantic longings, I was surprised to find that I could access more of my emotions. I was able to empathize with people more deeply.

What I didn't know before was that you can't selectively shut down. When I had suppressed my sexuality, I had to detach from my desires, my feelings, my intuition, my capacity for intimacy. That process of fragmentation inhibited my ability to truly know myself or connect with other people. When I opened myself up to love Amanda, I came alive. I felt like a whole human, with my mind, body, spirit, and emotions unleashed and integrated.

Then Monday mornings arrived each week, and I was alone with myself once again, grappling with questions of faith and meaning, wrestling with what to do with my life and days, spiraling further into a void. I never knew it was possible to be so happy and so sad at the same time.

19

I didn't tell anyone in my family that I was dating Amanda until a year into our relationship. My avoidant tendencies were bolstered by the space between us: I lived more than one thousand miles away from them, and the cultural distance was even greater. I felt like I had given them the first three decades of my life, devoting all of my energy to becoming the kind of person they wanted to be around, someone who made them proud. By the time I fully accepted my queer self, I was burned out. I no longer had the capacity to try to justify myself to people who weren't willing to do the work to understand me.

After we had been together for a year, though, I figured I should loop my family in so they wouldn't find out about us on the internet. They responded in predictable ways: my mother disapproved, Michael never responded, Kenny had questions, and my dad expressed cautious support with a reminder that my mom didn't know he approved, and we needed to keep it that way. My cousins, who I hadn't spoken to in more than a decade, found out on Facebook, and they were cool with it. The only relative who didn't know about me and my relationship was my grandma.

My maternal grandmother is a boisterous, ninety-four-year-old woman with German genes and Texas roots. Her given name is Dorothy, but I have only ever known her as Gugu. While I've always known her to be jolly and, to this day, I've never seen her without bright-red lipstick on, I've known two Gugus over the course of my life.

The first is the Gugu of my childhood. I experienced her then as a sort of fairy godmother: a benevolent woman who was larger than life, almost to the point of being out of reach. Like a fairy godmother, she always had yummy food prepared for us. Chocolate fudge, Rice Krispies treats, pumpkin pie, banana nut bread—these were just a few of the treats waiting for my brothers and me on her kitchen island when we made the four-hour drive to San Antonio. Then, of course, there were the casual meals that felt more like holiday feasts: mashed potatoes and gravy, green bean casserole, ham, turkey, stuffing, warm rolls, and without fail, both chocolate sheet cake and pecan pie. Gugu put a lot of love into the meals she prepared for us, which is another way of saying she let no grease go to waste. That was how she nurtured us. She didn't seem emotionally available, and we didn't go deep in conversation, but she spent hours hovering over hot stoves in small kitchens through eternal Texas summers as a way of showing love.

After I graduated high school, the road trips to visit Gugu ended. The relationship between my mom and Gugu had always been fragile, but after my grandpa died, it shattered. My grandma endured an unhappy marriage for most of her life, and within days of my grandpa passing, Gugu's high school sweetheart, Charles, saw his obituary in the newspaper and reached out to her to offer his condolences. They were dating within weeks, and he moved in with her a few months later. Gugu was high on love, and my mom was furious. She thought it was too soon. She worried they were having premarital sex.

She believed Charles was after her for her money (Gugu was not rich). After that, we only saw Gugu about once a year, when our whole family was together for the holidays.

The second Gugu I've known was the one I met in my early thirties. After I told my family about Amanda, it occurred to me that my mom probably ranted about it to my grandma and that I hadn't even come out to Gugu. So I sent her a long letter and said something like "Oh, by the way, I'm gay! And in love! Here's a post I wrote about Amanda—let me know if you ever want to meet her."

Gugu wrote me a letter the next week that said, "Oh, Julie, I'm so glad you've found love and that you're happy. Amanda sounds like a wonderful woman. I would love to meet her! When can you come for a visit?"

I set the letter down in disbelief. Not a single family member had expressed interest in meeting Amanda. I had resigned myself to Gugu's disappointment before giving her a chance to surprise me. And there she was, my then ninety-two-year-old grandma, a lifelong Republican, enthusiastically welcoming me and Amanda into her life. She signed that letter the same way she's signed each one since: "God loves you and so do I."

"Babe!" I yelled from the kitchen. "You're not gonna believe this! Look at Gugu's letter!"

I jumped into the bed next to Amanda, and she pressed her head against my cheek as she read the letter. She had spent hours listening to me mourn my family's rejection of us, so she understood the weight of Gugu's response. Amanda's always said she prefers kids and old people—everyone else is hit or miss.

"Let's book flights now!" she said, pulling up the calendar on her phone. Three weeks later, we were on a plane to San

Antonio, where I would see Gugu for the first time in years and finally get to introduce Amanda to someone in my family.

When we drove up to Gugu's house in our rental car, she was standing in the window of the front room, watching for us. We turned into the driveway of the white house I had visited countless times as a kid, the American flag still waving on the front lawn. Gugu met us at the door, and when we hugged, I was surprised by how much smaller she felt in my arms than she had been in my imagination. She felt fragile.

She pulled Amanda in close and gave a warm, hearty greeting and then said, "Let me show you two to your room." We understood she was signaling full acceptance of us as a couple—*respect* for us as a couple. She wasn't going to police our relationship by putting us in separate rooms.

Amanda and I followed her down the hallway to the only bedroom downstairs, where she told us to get settled.

"Are you all hungry?" she asked. "I didn't know whether you would've eaten, so I made some food for you if you want it."

"Gugu, you didn't have to do that!" I yelled. Of course she made food. "We're starving, though—we'll be right there."

Amanda and I gushed about how precious Gugu was as we changed into sweatpants and T-shirts. Then we walked through the dim living room to the kitchen, past framed photos of her and Charles and Christmas cards from my brothers' families leaned up against old books. The photos were different, but everything else was exactly as I remembered it. For the first time, Amanda was getting to physically enter into a scene from my childhood. She got to be in the rooms and meet a person who was part of forming me into the woman she now loved.

"Do you all like egg rolls?" Gugu asked.

"Of course we do!" I said. "Who doesn't like egg rolls?"

"And you both eat meat, I hope? I've got some sesame chicken for us."

We were vegetarians, but there was no universe in which we weren't eating the food Gugu prepared for us.

"Absolutely. But Gugu, let us help! You don't need to do all of this for us."

"No, you two sit down at the table—this kitchen's too small for three anyway."

The table was already set in the living room, so we sat down and talked to her through a large window in the wall between us.

"Would you like some wine?" she asked. "I've got a bottle of red wine here in the refrigerator—why don't we all have a glass?"

Alcohol was strictly forbidden from family gatherings when I was a kid, so Gugu and I had never shared a drink. This was another sign to me that she understood I was an adult now, capable of making my own choices about right and wrong.

It occurred to me that I had never really known Gugu, and she hadn't known me. Throughout my childhood, we were always performing, being the people we had to be in order to keep the peace around family members who had strong opinions about how everyone else was supposed to live. Now I was finally getting to meet my ninety-two-year-old grandma, and she was a treasure.

Gugu brought each dish to the table with trembling hands, and while it was different than the homemade feasts of my childhood, I had never felt so loved by a meal. There was such tenderness in her desire to feed us once again. We ate honey-glazed carrots, pepperoni pizza rolls, egg rolls, and sesame chicken with thankful hearts. We drank red wine together like we were sharing Communion at Gugu's dining room table.

The next morning, Amanda and I woke up to the sound of Fox News commentators raging in the living room. Gugu's hearing was almost entirely gone, so she likely couldn't hear the discussion, but it was familiar for her, and it was a connection to the broader world. Amanda got out of bed and went to visit with Gugu while I laid there basking in the moment: my wife-to-be and my grandma, chatting away like in-laws do.

Over the course of the weekend, I learned all about Gugu's relationship with Charles. They had been together for more than fifteen years by this point. He was ninety-five and had to move to a nursing home in the Dallas area, but they still spoke every morning at eight and every evening at eight. You would've thought he still lived with her based on the way she left things. There were Post-it notes inside kitchen cabinets that told her she was beautiful and notes on her bathroom mirror addressed to "my darling." When she saw how we swooned over her and Charles's love story, she shuffled over to an antique chest and pulled out a stack of cards and letters.

"I policed myself a little before y'all came and hid these love notes, but look here at all these letters he's written to me!"

I thought my heart might burst out of my chest. Both of us faced judgment for loving the people we loved, and we both knew the pressure of having to negotiate relationships with family when they don't approve of your partner. That day we offered each other an acceptance we had each longed for: to be seen in love and to have that love celebrated.

I had wanted so badly for there to be a bridge between the family I came from and the one I was building. I didn't want to lead a life disconnected from the person I had always been. I needed someone who knew me then to see me now, fully out and in love with Amanda, and I wanted them to acknowledge that I was the same Julie, yet somehow stronger, more tender-hearted, more whole. Gugu gave me that gift.

My grandma told stories throughout the weekend that I had never heard before. She talked about living in Germany and Iran when my grandpa was in the army. She showed us a painting that was given to her by a woman she had been friends with in the 1950s in her hometown of Brenham, Texas. She talked about the neighborhood church she had been a part of for decades. We even took her down to the Riverwalk one afternoon, which was a terrible idea because it required a lot of walking in the heat, but she put makeup on and wore a plaid shirt that matched mine. As we walked along the river, hand in hand, I felt the sun on my skin and noticed strangers' faces lighting up when they walked by us in our matching shirts: I was clearly my grandmother's granddaughter, and I couldn't have been more proud.

20

In the summer of 2017, Amanda and I were in Italy with a group of friends when we stole away for some time alone in Venice. The morning after we arrived, we left our hotel early, intent on doing what everyone recommended we do in Venice: get lost. After wandering along the canals for a few hours, we stopped at a quaint café on the water and got a table next to a basket of bright-red flowers that hung over the river. Amanda ordered a bottle of champagne, and I knew right then that she was going to propose. Why had I worn a T-shirt and jogging shorts for a romantic day in Venice?

The waiter brought the champagne to our table, showed the label to Amanda, and then held the bottle with his right hand while twisting the cork with his left. The champagne exploded from the bottle and showered me, head to toe. I felt like I had just won the World Cup and my teammates had shaken bottles of bubbly to douse me for the sake of celebration.

Then Amanda asked me to marry her. Still dripping with champagne, I said, "Yes! Oh my God, yes!" She cried, we kissed, and we toasted to our love with the champagne that was left in the bottle. We spent the rest of the day floating through the canals and then reunited with our friends for a celebratory dinner that evening.

We closed on our first home and moved in a few weeks after our trip to Italy. In typical lesbian style, our family expanded about a month later with the adoption of our first cat. Amanda was well aware that I spent an excessive amount of time scrolling through kitten photos on social media. I knew all the dogs that lived in our old building, and when we ran into someone familiar that Amanda couldn't quite place, I identified them by their furry friends: "Oh, that's Chewy's dad!"

Amanda didn't want a pet, but she really wanted a digital baby grand piano, so we made a deal: Amanda would hold off on buying a piano until we got a kitten. Then one night, Amanda did some late-night shopping, and I woke up the next day to her confession. As providence would have it, our bestie, Sharon, sent us a Facebook post that afternoon about a precious kitten at a shelter in West Virginia. Two women on a road trip from Ohio to Maryland heard a high-pitched meow coming from beneath their car when they stopped for gas. Sure enough, the kitten who would eventually be known as Prince was curled up in the spare tire underneath their car.

Within minutes, Amanda was texting Sharon: "We'll take the cat. I did some late-night shopping and bought a piano. How do we get the cat?"

After a few hours with Prince, Amanda was so infatuated that she took a week off work to be with him. He purred and snuggled us. He kneaded our stomachs and turned our legs into jungle gyms. One of my all-time favorite photos is a snapshot of Prince rubbing the top of his head into the bottom of Amanda's chin. Before we knew it, our new home had more cat furniture than human furniture. Prince had a miniature velvet couch, two cat towers, dozens of jingle balls, and a subscription to Temptations (his favorite treats).

Amanda's affection for Prince made me swoon. Wasn't that the trajectory of love? When two humans give themselves to one another, their love expands and creates an energy that welcomes others into a place of belonging. Love is not finite. It's not like a pizza that has a limited number of square inches to be divided up and consumed. It's not like the amount of time set for an exam, with only a certain number of minutes that can be allotted to each essay question before they eat into time that could go to another. Love is a renewable resource that multiplies ad infinitum when we tune into it and nurture it.

From my theological background, I understood on a cognitive level that our love for God, rather than competing with our love for people, is the source of our love for them. On another level, I understood marriage in a similar light. The union created the possibility for new life, whether through procreation, adoption, or hospitality. That gay love functions in a similar way should not have surprised me, but it was a revelation, nonetheless. Of course my relationship with Amanda deepened my love for our friends. Of course our love for one another increased our capacity to nurture new life: the wisdom, the sensitivities, the resources are multiplied and amplified when fused together.

Amanda and I were in no rush to get married. In a way, we felt like we were already living into the commitment we had made to share our lives together.

"Maybe we'll go to the courthouse with a few of our besties," we often thought out loud. "We can have a small, private ceremony, and then someday we'll have a party with friends who want to celebrate us."

It wasn't until I officiated a wedding for a lesbian couple in Mexico that Amanda caught a vision for the wedding she wanted. From the moment we arrived at the reception, she started gushing: "Babe, I want to have the ceremony our love deserves! I want it to be in a *church* and for *everyone* to celebrate our love!"

"We can talk about it," I said halfheartedly. "Let's just enjoy the reception tonight."

"But I want a *wedding*," she insisted.

"Okay, okay. We'll chat about it later."

I figured it would pass once the thrill of the moment wore off.

Then, a few weeks later, the vicar at the Washington National Cathedral offered to marry us in their church.

"Can you believe it, babe? The nation's cathedral! We can get married where Martin Luther King Jr. gave his last sermon!"

"It's a beautiful church," I conceded. "It's also incredibly expensive to get married there."

"We only get married once! Don't worry about the money. I promise I'll take care of it."

I told her I was open to it as long as we wouldn't go into debt over it. A few days later, Amanda called me over to the couch and pulled up a spreadsheet with a budget that outlined exactly how we would pay for the wedding. The math added up. And the cathedral was breathtaking. I ran out of reasons to say no. Eventually, I found good reasons to say yes: We loved Rev. Dana Corsello, the priest who offered to marry us, and the cathedral had been a spiritual home to us during our time in DC. It was the community that led Amanda back to the church when they enthusiastically celebrated the gifts of queer people. I was also moved by the idea of getting married in a church. While I believed God's presence was everywhere, as near to us in the mountains as the altar of a cathedral, I saw the potential for a kind of redemption: What might it feel like to make our vows in the very place where our love was once seen as a disgrace?

"Okay!" I said with genuine enthusiasm in the kitchen one evening. "Let's get married at the cathedral."

The Episcopal Church breathed new life into my faith. In most services, the congregation reads Scripture aloud and sings hymns that have been refined and passed down over the course of thousands of years. A priest delivers a short sermon, which is a nice contrast to the central role of the sermon in other traditions that often sets the stage for celebrity pastors and reaffirms their authority. We recite liturgy together written and spoken by the saints of old. And when we do that, I feel swept into a current that's been running for much longer than I've been alive. All I have to do is immerse myself in the water, and it carries me when I struggle to find my way in the faith.

The tradition doesn't insist on each member rationally assenting to various theological claims. Faith doesn't work that way. It's more like a rhythm you step into in hope that the practices will form you into a more gracious person who's driven by love over fear.

Alongside the Episcopal Church, I also found a spiritual home with the Newbigin House of Studies, an affiliate of the Graduate Theological Union in Berkeley. Newbigin House is a progressive theological education program housed in City Church San Francisco, a vibrant, Evangelical-adjacent church that moved to fully affirm LGBTQ people shortly before I did. A few months after I left Wheaton, City Church invited me out to speak. And from that point on, they looked for opportunities to partner with me.

The education I received at Newbigin House deepened my understanding of the ways that racism and sexism were woven into the fabric of the tradition I was raised in. We read theologians who had traditionally been excluded by the largely white and male gatekeepers of "orthodoxy." We read books by historians, sociologists, and political scientists—thinkers who shed light on the structural injustices that created the vast inequalities we see in our society today.

It was the first Christian community I had been a part of that helped me understand sin as a corporate issue rather than simply individual acts of moral failure. When we looked at the ways European Christians baptized violence in the new world, and when I learned how white Evangelicals used the Bible to justify the enslavement of African American people, I began to distinguish among different kinds of Christianities (or at least different communities who lay claim to the Christian label). I understood that the Christianity I had grown up in was the faith of empire. It was a religion that sought financial gain and cultural dominance. It was a means by which to gain power.

Through our studies at Newbigin House, I saw a different kind of Christianity that invites us to practice theological humility. It's a faith that asks us to interrogate our complicity in the inequities in our communities and commit to using our time, energy, and resources to work for justice for people who are oppressed.

As I read Scripture with this kind of Christianity in mind, it was immediately more resonant for me. When I read the Gospels and try to imagine whom Jesus would prioritize if he were in our world today, I believe he would be with immigrants and refugees, not the gatekeepers of evangelicalism. I believe he would side with the transgender middle schooler over the fearmongering lawmaker, and the homeless person battling mental health issues over those who rush by them with fear and judgment.

This kind of Christianity isn't partisan. No political party can honestly lay claim to Christianity. We are called to love our neighbors, though. We're urged to empathize with those who suffer and seek to rectify the conditions that caused that suffering. At Newbigin House and City Church, I was exposed to people compelled by their faith to alleviate suffering in the world around them. I caught a vision for what it might look like to lean into my faith in a way that both challenged and healed me.

My faith looks a lot different now than it did when I was part of accountability groups where we confessed how often we masturbated each week. My faith has more room for mystery and more questions than answers. I don't know what to make of many theological claims related to invisible things. I have not made peace with death.

I'm content to leave a lot of room for mystery and to engage in spiritual practices that might not totally make sense on a rational level. I believe Christian practices have the potential to form me into a more humble, generous, faithful person, so I keep showing up, hoping to be surprised by God.

o o o

Besides my grandmother, I hadn't seen anyone in my family since the Christmas after I left Wheaton. Two or three times a year, I emailed them to share about a big development in my life: that I was moving to DC, or seeing Amanda, or engaged to be married. Most of the emails went unanswered, but my dad and I kept in touch. When we spoke, he always said he missed me, but it would cause too much disruption at home for him to see me. He hadn't changed much from the years when he hugged me after lunches and then reminded me that if my mom asked, the meeting "never happened."

Then in July of 2018, my dad broke from his lifelong pattern of setting his needs aside to placate the strong personalities in his life. "What about Mom?" I asked when he called to say he wanted to visit me and finally meet Amanda.

"She's going to be upset, but she'll have to just accept it."

My dad got in his silver Honda Civic in Dallas, Texas, and drove all the way up to DC to stay with us for a week and a half. He arrived two days after Amanda and I returned from a trip to Thailand, when we were jet-lagged and six weeks away from the wedding we were planning. We gave him our undivided attention anyway. We toured the Capitol with a friend who worked in the House. We cruised down the Potomac on a tour boat that focused on historical sites along the water. We threw a party at our place to introduce him to our best friends and neighbors. But the most memorable parts of his visit, by far, were our evening conversations.

Every night, my dad helped himself to a generous glass of chardonnay and sat in the same seat on our brown leather couch with his legs crossed at the knee. Amanda and I snuggled up on the love seat across from him and listened to him talk for hours. I had never seen him talk so freely before, waving his hands and raising his voice as he bemoaned the state of politics in Texas. He told stories about his life that I'd never heard before—about facing age discrimination when he pursued a PhD after retirement and got stonewalled at his dissertation. He reminisced about his time living abroad when he was in the army, how he still wonders if he should've stayed in Germany instead of coming back to the states to go to college. He told me all about the people my nieces and nephews had become in the years since I'd last seen them.

And most nights, after a few glasses of wine, he found his way to memories of us. He relived moments like the decision to send me to Living Hope—"I know your life has not been easy, sugar," he choked out. "You've always been such a sweet girl, and I wish things had gone differently with you. I do."

With tears streaming down his cheeks, he told me that I was special, that he believed in me, and that I had always been a source of light and joy to the people around me. He said these things with the emotional conviction of a person on their deathbed. And as he shared, Amanda met him in that emotional place. She leaned forward and nodded along, often crying with him as he lamented the suffering I endured in my younger years.

As they cried together, I shifted in my seat, crossed my arms, rubbed my face with my hand like I had an imaginary beard. Obviously, it was nice to hear my dad acknowledge some of the sad truths of my life. I appreciated his affirmation of my gifts. I understood we were supposed to be having a moment: there was my seventy-five-year-old father, frailer than I'd ever seen him, opening his tender heart up to me and my wife-to-be. After fifty years of marriage, he finally stood up for me to my mom and acknowledged the ways he'd failed me.

He said things I had longed to hear my whole life, words that reconcile and heal. Yet I was unmoved. I felt like a distant observer bearing witness to a moment that theoretically should have affected me, but I couldn't help feeling like those emotionally intense connections had to be earned. I had thirty years of experiences that left me wounded. It was going to take more than a week for me to be emotionally vulnerable with my dad, especially around such tender issues.

It wasn't until I waved goodbye as he drove away in his silver Honda Civic that I could finally take it in: My dad saw me. He had always seen me. It takes a lot of courage to break out of the well-worn paths we create in our relationships. At the age of seventy-five, my dad showed me people can change. I wasn't able to match his vulnerability at the time, but I received his words and treasured them, knowing I would look back on that week with gratitude for the rest of my life.

Early on in his visit, I asked my dad if he thought there was any chance he could make it to our wedding. Amanda quickly chimed in, offering to pay for his flight and hotel if he would make the trip.

"I'd sure love to be there," he said, nodding his head from side to side, "but I'm afraid your mom would never let it happen."

I closed my eyes so I wouldn't roll them.

But on his last night in DC, my dad told Amanda and me that he couldn't remember the last time he felt as happy as he had that week. He said he hadn't felt so free to be himself since he was in Germany in the army. I felt like I was watching him come out of a different kind of closet, much like I had seen Gugu feel permission to bring her whole self forward in the presence of our queer love.

"If the offer is still on the table," my dad said with conviction, "I'd like to come to the wedding."

The week before our wedding, Amanda and I were at brunch when we received a call from the dean of the cathedral: "Hi, Amanda, this is Randy Hollerith from the Washington National Cathedral. Do you have a minute?"

"Sure!" she said as she stepped outside to escape the noisy restaurant.

"I'm sure you're aware that Senator John McCain passed away earlier this week."

"Yeah," Amanda said. "We've actually been wondering when his memorial service would be, since we figured it would take place at the cathedral."

"Well, that's what I'm calling about. We've been waiting to share details about the service with reporters because we wanted to talk to you first. Senator McCain's memorial service is going to be on Saturday morning, the same day as your wedding. We tried to work with the family to have the service on another day, but then members of Congress got involved, and there was a big push to have it on Saturday. The main reason I'm calling is to tell you that your wedding is every bit as important to us as the Senator's memorial service. It'll be a quick turnaround, but we'll have all hands on deck to make sure everything goes as smoothly as possible. Public ceremonies are a part of our ministry here, but you're family. We want your special day to be everything you dreamed it would be."

We had anxiously followed the news all week long. "Will they cancel our wedding?" we wondered to each other as we realized McCain's funeral would likely be on Saturday. "What will we do if they cancel it? Most of our friends are flying in from out of town—we can't just bump it to the following week." It never occurred to us that the church would consider our wedding, a marriage between two little-known lesbians, as equally important as a senator's memorial service, where three former presidents would be in attendance.

Amanda thanked Dean Randy and then returned to our table to share the news. Before the wedding day had even arrived, we already experienced a surprising sense of healing. I had been wary of a big wedding for many reasons: I didn't want to play into our culture's obsession with marriage and the nuclear family, as if we're incomplete until we find the mythical "one." I didn't want to contribute to the rampant consumerism around the wedding industry. I didn't want all the attention. I just wanted to be married to Amanda and then go about the ordinary rhythms of sharing our lives with one another. And yet, it was still affirming to be included and prioritized by institutions that play a significant role in shaping our social imagination.

A whole lot of people take it upon themselves to offer unsolicited advice in the lead-up to a wedding. I usually listened politely and then passed the suggestions along to Amanda. There was, however, one piece of advice that I held on to for myself: "When you walk down the aisle," someone told me, "make it a point to connect with as many of your guests as possible. Don't just stare straight ahead at the officiant. Allow yourself to take it all in."

I thought about that as Amanda and I stood in the wing in the cathedral on that Saturday evening in September, waiting to walk down the aisle. We lined up behind our wedding party, both taking deep, focused breaths to avoid passing out

from nerves. Then our song began. We walked to the center
of the cathedral and turned left to begin the long march, hand
in hand, to the high altar. A woman named Imani Grace, from
the cathedral's gospel choir, sang Beyoncé's "Ave Maria," and
for the first part of our walk, I poured all of my energy into
putting one foot in front of the other.

Then we entered the high altar, where our guests were
seated in wooden pews that faced each other, and one by one,
our gazes aligned: Mrs. Jarvis, my substitute teacher in high
school; Jason, my big brother from Living Hope; my ride or
die, Myles, who had come out as trans since the weekend we
shared in San Francisco; my Oak Park family; my Oklahoma
cousins whom Gugu sent in her place; my dad.

Each time I caught someone's gaze, I held on to it and
nodded as if to say, "We made it. You *saw* me at a desperate
time, when neither of us could imagine this moment, and you
moved with me through all the twists and turns until we made
it to this place where I'm finally free."

Every time I made that connection with someone, their
eyes filled with tears, and they nodded back. They knew how
hard I fought to get to this place. I was so overwhelmed by
the love I felt from the people who had carried me to that
moment that I thought I might fall to the floor and weep.

Amanda and I made it to the altar, where we were relieved
to be in the warm presence of our priest, Dana. She led us
through the traditional wedding liturgy: we said our vows, she
blessed our union, we kissed, people cheered, and then we
celebrated Communion together.

The flow of our ceremony was the same as almost all
the weddings I had attended, yet it was nothing like them.
Our wedding felt triumphant, like it was about something

much bigger than me and Amanda. It felt like sunlight bursting through clouds after a storm, like good news from a surgeon, like a victory song after the underdog beats the odds.

It wasn't until after the wedding, when I looked through our photos, that I understood the depth of the redemption I felt that day. For the first time in any formal or social situation, I had chosen to wear a sleeveless dress. Prominently displayed in all of the close-up shots of us together were the scars on my shoulders from my years in conversion therapy, when I turned to self-harm to cope with the pain. They had been a source of shame throughout my entire adult life. Every time I wore workout clothes or went for a swim, I was self-conscious, anxiously waiting for someone to ask about my scars. *There's no way to save face*, I often thought when I was forced to go sleeveless. *No way to spin this that could allow me to pass as socially acceptable. What kind of maniac burns her own body?*

The day I married Amanda, however, I bore my scars with pride. All those years before, I thought they told a story about a neurotic queer who was broken and deranged. I thought they were a symbol of my failure. Something shifted when I opened my body to love, when I allowed it to be seen and held and caressed. I finally understood the scars told a story of a girl who was born into a system that tried to kill her, one that demanded she change, hide, make herself smaller and smaller, until she disappeared.

And by the grace of God, I survived.

21

Every Saturday morning, Amanda makes french toast, and we play dominoes while we listen to music. I'm tone-deaf, but I sing anyway. Lately, I've been singing songs from the *Hamilton* soundtrack, substituting our cats' names for the founding fathers as if no one else is around to hear me sing something so silly and off-key. The game goes on long after we finish eating, well into our second and third cups of coffee. We take short breaks when Prince's brother Toby jumps on our kitchen table or knocks over his water bowl. In a tone of voice reserved exclusively for our cats, Amanda will say, "He just needs some attention!" Then she'll get on all fours to play with him or she'll run up and down the hallway with a jingling cat toy while Toby chases after her. *What a miracle*, I think to myself with a smile. *This is all I ever wanted.*

Those moments can give the impression that I got the fairy-tale ending, but the truth is more complicated. Shortly after we married, I started asking questions about myself and my relationships that most people work through in their twenties—questions I didn't get the chance to explore when I was in conversion therapy. Working through my extensive sexual and relational baggage after we were married has been painful for both of us. At the same time, I feel pressure to excel at marriage, since we had to fight so hard just to get to this place. I told a friend about this recently, and he reminded me that marriage equality just gave us equal opportunity to wrestle with the same things straight couples have been wrestling with for centuries, with the added layer of decades of trauma thrown on top. That's true of our first few years of marriage, even as Amanda and I have also felt immense joy and grown deeper in love together.

The rhythms of our life now allow for more reflection than I had the first few years after my ejection from evangelicalism. Those were the years of falling in love, moving to DC, buying our first home, planning a wedding. There was always something to look forward to when I needed a distraction from the sadness that was just beneath the surface. Now I have space to sit with my grief, my questions, my longing for reconciliation, or at least a sense of closure that may never come.

In quiet moments, my mind drifts to the past. When I'm reflective, or even when I have good news to share, I often wish I could pick up the phone and talk to Ricky the way we used to. Sometimes he shows up in my dreams, telling me he's disappointed with me but that he still loves me. His wife, Merlinda, died from cancer earlier this year, and it was the first time someone I had been really close to died while we were still on bad terms. I always imagined broken relationships were mended before people passed away, that we apologized to one another and offered forgiveness and then held one another's hands in those final moments. I didn't know that sometimes you get a text saying someone you used to love died, and when you look through your phone to read the last conversation you had, you confirm they were words of condemnation.

I bought Ricky a card to send him, and every day I thought about what to write to him, but I never could bring myself to write the card. I didn't know how to open up communication with him in a sincere way without also letting him know I have a lot of unresolved anger. You can't qualify your statements in a letter like that, though: "We obviously have a lot of baggage we need to work through, but I wanted to say I'm sorry your wife died."

No one wants that card.

But he keeps showing up in my dreams. I often imagine letters I would write to him telling him I know, beyond a shadow of a doubt, that he loved me. I would tell him I know he had good intentions and that I will never forget the way he cared for me at a time when I was incredibly vulnerable. I would write about the difference between intention and impact, how you can mean well but be part of a toxic system and perpetuate harmful narratives that devastate the lives of people you set out to love. I want to be able to tell him I forgive him, even though I'm not exactly sure how the process of forgiveness works.

Here's why I haven't been able to write that letter: Ricky is still the executive director of Living Hope. Each week, more than a hundred people gather to hear him preach about how they're inherently broken because of the way they were wired to love. The organization continues to grow: they now have over 10,000 people on their online forums. He pushes harmful narratives about sex and gender, often to parents of trans and queer kids, who then push that narrative on their vulnerable children.

Ricky speaks at Evangelical megachurches, like the ones my brothers attend, sharing a polished version of reparative therapy talking points that have been denounced by all the major psychological and medical groups in the country. I can forgive him in my heart, but I don't know how to move toward a restored relationship with him while he preaches a message that ultimately harms LGBTQ people.

Things are further complicated since I've shared about some of the controversial practices we engaged in at Living Hope. He poured thousands of hours into me—listening to me, consoling me, encouraging me, baking cakes for my birthdays, showing up to my sports games, snapping photos at my graduations—I can imagine it might seem unfair for me to publicly divulge some of the most controversial moments that happened over the course of our decade together.

I've shared openly about it because it's the only way to describe the specific ways in which a system breaks a person down and makes them hate themselves. I don't know how else to help people understand how an organization that claims to be about discipleship and grace and "walking with people toward Jesus" can make a person loathe their body, make them want to set themselves on fire in an attempt to burn the perceived impurities away.

Ricky is a complicated human being who deserves to be understood as such. Also, the vulnerable queer people trying to imagine a future where they don't hate themselves deserve better than the false hope offered to them at Living Hope. I do not apologize for telling the truth about what happens in communities that divide families and crush queer people.

Still, I keep the card for Ricky in the drawer of my nightstand. I hope someday I can send it. I hope he wakes up to the harm his work causes and begins to imagine new possibilities for the queer people that I know he loves. I hope he'll come to see that God's family is much bigger than he allowed himself to believe and that Jesus will walk with him into a new space if he's ever moved to embrace the beauty of the queer community. I hope someday I'll get the chance to tell him all that's broken between us can be mended.

I haven't seen my mother or brothers since Amanda and I got engaged. Since all of my crucial developmental years unfolded in a fundamentalist system that was hell-bent on misunderstanding and misrepresenting people like me, I feel like I'm to blame for my family's dissolution. That feeling is beneath the level of rationality. I know our separation is the result of pastors who excommunicate queer members, books that tell parents to cut off their gay children, and leaders who convince them that my gayness is an act of willful disobedience from which I need to repent in order for us to be reconciled. Still, I find ways to blame myself.

I've sent countless emails to my family telling them I would relish the opportunity to see them if they're ever open to meeting Amanda and seeing me as I truly am. Most of them go unanswered. My best guess is that they're trying to figure out what to do with me: What do they tell the kids? What do they do with their fears? What if they love Amanda? We're all busy, anyway. It's easier to tend to the things that fit neatly within the worlds we've built for ourselves. Most days, I don't let it get to me. I tell myself I did what I had to do to survive, that I only wish I'd done it sooner.

Then there are the days when I face my family's story with clear-eyed sadness. On those days, I will go for a long run beside the stream in Rock Creek Park, far away from the noise and bustle of the city. I'll play the music that made up the soundtrack of the years we spent together, and suddenly my body is transported back into the passenger's seat of my mom's 1980s-style Suburban, singing "I Got You Babe" with Sonny and Cher, believing with all our hearts the lyrics were written for us. I remember that my mom's only aspiration in life was to be a good mom. I reflect on the sacrifices she made for me. Tears stream down my cheeks as I run faster and faster, imagining the agony my mom must feel about our estrangement, how she replays our history over and over, wondering if there was another way, pleading with God to lead me back to a place where I would repent for the way in which I'm wired to love.

I cannot and will not do that. So I let my heart crack open as I imagine us both reaching out for one another, unable to join hands because we came up in a system that said a parent's love for God demands they reject their queer child.

I believe we will be reconciled. Even though we haven't seen each other in years and don't talk often, my mom still occasionally sends me care packages. Last year, she sent me socks made by a brand named Prince because she thought it would be cute for me to have socks with my cat's name on the toes. A lot of care goes into the process of sending a package: she thought of me when she saw the socks, stood in line to purchase them, wrapped them in tissue paper, decorated it with stickers, drove to the post office, waited in line, and paid for it to be delivered to me in DC. She doesn't know how to interact with me, and she's afraid to meet Amanda, but the socks give me hope.

It's strange to be on this side of the line Evangelicals drew to demarcate who's in and who's out, who's good and who's bad.

I think of how Ricky described people like me as having "given in to their flesh" and "gone to the dark side." I remember him imagining himself as the father in the story of the prodigal son, waiting with his arms wide open for those of us who are lost to come home.

Here's what I couldn't have imagined then: The morning after I wrote the post professing my support for same-sex relationships, effectively ending my relationship with evangelicalism, I buried my head in my hands and prayed to ask where God was in all of the chaos. Reporters reached out for comments. Friends texted their disappointment. Conservatives wrote glib takedowns. I no longer had a job, and I feared I had disqualified myself from the work I was made to do. With my head in my hands and tears streaming down my face, I asked God to be near, to help me make sense of it all.

In that moment, I had a vision in which I was walking down a dirt road.

I do not have visions, I thought to myself. *This is not God. This is my imagination trying to make sense of my sadness.*

The scene moved along anyway, despite my disbelief: When I dragged my beaten-down body around the corner and looked up ahead, I saw an old home with a wraparound porch and the outline of a person looking toward me. With determination, I put one foot in front of the other, gaining strength the closer I got, until the figure in the distance started running toward me. Their jog eventually turned into a sprint; they were leaping at times, almost dancing as they drew near. Finally, we met, and I collapsed into their arms.

"Welcome home!" they cried, taking a step back to look at me.

"All these years, I've been waiting for you to come to me as you are—not the version of yourself you thought you were supposed to be, but the person beneath the religious facade. And now here you are, all pretense stripped away, in the body I knit together, with a soft and open heart, home at last."

Was that a vision from God? Or was it my imagination seeking comfort in a familiar story, redemptive in its reinterpretation? I'm no longer interested in that question. I've come to believe religion and spirituality have the power to harm and the power to heal. I'm less concerned with what's behind the force that nurtures extravagant love than I am with its manifestation. What we know with certainty is that every day, we are faced with choices about how to live among our neighbors. Imagine how we'll remake the world if we all choose love.

ACKNOWLEDGMENTS

I could not possibly have written this book if it weren't for the community that carried me every step of the way, especially Christine Folch, Larycia Hawkins, and Carey Wallace. I'm immensely thankful for their friendship when I lived these stories, their support as I've healed, their feedback on this book, our group text, our Zoom calls, and the way we share fears, joys, and sorrows. You all have been God's grace to me.

This book would have been infinitely less compelling if it weren't for the feedback I received from Kate Bowler, Brent Bailey, Steve Slagg, and Jess Devaney. Thank you for gently challenging me to dig deeper, making me laugh in the margins, and helping me feel a sense of possibility around this story, even when writing days were sad and discouraging. You all made me a better writer and person through this process.

I'm not sure my faith would've survived these last few years if it weren't for the spiritual guidance and friendship I've received from Peter Choi and the Newbigin House of Studies. Thank you for modeling humility and integrity in your spiritual leadership. You give me hope for faith communities.

I'm deeply thankful to my agents, Claudia Cross and Sonali Chanchani, for taking a chance on me and this book early on. You are a delight to work with, and you're incredibly good at what you do. I'm also thankful to Lil Copan, my editor, for the warm spirit, critical eye, and general wisdom you brought to every stage of the writing process.

I believe a large part of writing a good memoir is about being a good person, and a few dear friends have made me a much better person these last few years: Rebecca Lee Funk, Daniel Correa, Sharon Rose, and Kirsten Powers, thank you for being the kinds of friends who are closer than family.

Finally, there is no universe in which this book could've been written without Amanda. She kept the lights on and lifted my spirits while I stared at blank documents on my computer. She held me when I wept while reading early drafts of the book and then helped me process the complicated feelings that surfaced. Beyond being my biggest champion as a writer, Amanda, you taught me how to love. You make me stronger and softer at the same time, both of which I needed to write this book with grace. You are my forever family, and I can't wait to see who we become as we write new stories together.

NOTES

Chapter 2

8   **"nurturing and defending the God-ordained institution"**: "Our Mission," Focus on the Family, accessed November 24, 2020, https://tinyurl.com/yxv8du33.

Chapter 8

87   **"the most divisive issue of our day"**: Associated Press, "Robertson Letter Attacks Feminists," *New York Times*, August 26, 1992, https://tinyurl.com/y399rugq.

87   **"AIDS is not just God's punishment"**: Jerry Falwell, letter on keeping *Old-Time Gospel Hour* on air, August 13, 1981, Resource Center LGBTQ Collection of the UNT Libraries, UNT Libraries Special Collections, Portal to Texas History, https://tinyurl.com/y3rrqskl.